The Three Chefs especially wish to thank _CityLine_ producer Chrissie Rejman and host Tracy Moore for their inspiration and their support of the Three Chefs specials over these many years, for their encouragement and ideas—and for telling us to get it all down in a book!

We're proud to be a part of _CityLine_, Canada's longest-running lifestyle show. We know just how many fans love Tracy's show because they tell us so, wherever we go. Chrissie, Tracy, and every one of the fabulous _CityLine_ team have shown us the fine art of talking and cooking on camera, connecting us with audiences all across the country. Everyone at _CityLine_ contributes to the fun we have on Three Chefs.

You know what they say about too many cooks. Well, don't believe it. When the three of us get together at the _CityLine_ studios, it's more than just the highlight of the month: it's the most fun anyone can have before lunch!

—Jason, Massimo, and Michael

passion for excellence

Like many of you, I know each of the Three Chefs, with their
reputation for good fun and their ongoing culinary adventures.
Their television specials, in which they show their many loyal
fans how to make great fresh food and try out new ideas in the
kitchen, are but one small part of their very busy lives.

As you will see in this book, these three gentlemen are pro-
fessionals who have trained to the very highest standards, and
who bring a passionate commitment to everything they do.

Of the three, I know Michael Bonacini best of all, of course.
When we met some 20 years ago, Michael was chef at one
of Toronto's top restaurants, and I was a local restaurateur.
Our connection was immediate. We both shared a passion for
good food, great service, and gracious dining. So we struck up
a partnership that has been vibrant and filled with exciting
enterprises—for the two of us, for the colleagues we have been
fortunate to work with, and for the many diners we have been
proud to welcome to our restaurants.

Our first venture together was Jump, one of the earliest
upscale eateries in Toronto's financial district. We took a
chance on an unlikely location in a bank tower atrium because
we had a vision of creating something big, bold, and completely

new in the city. Michael's food was right on the mark—rooted in tradition, but each dish was given a fresh, modern spin. In fact, many of those original Jump dishes have gone on to become Oliver & Bonacini classics, like the mushroom soup, the spinach pecan salad, and the baby back ribs.

Our O&B partnership has since grown to include Canoe, critically considered one of Canada's best dining experiences; Auberge du Pommier, offering classic French fine dining; Biff's Bistro for casual Parisian-style dining; Oliver & Bonacini Café Grill for approachable metropolitan food; and our landmark new restaurants, O&B Canteen and Luma at the TIFF Bell Lightbox, home of the Toronto International Film Festival.

Knowing Michael as I do, it doesn't surprise me that he, Massimo, and Jason have come together as such a phenomenal team because they are much the same in life as they are on television. They are witty, sporty, mischievous, and incredibly creative. Each is fired up by new ideas. Most importantly, they are consummate pros—in the kitchen and in the dining room. They have a legion of followers amongst the cooks and servers whom they have inspired, mentored, and developed over the years.

I hope you get many years of enjoyment out of the recipes in this book—and keep an eye out for the O&B classics!

—Peter Oliver

View from the top: The view over the city from Canoe, the O&B restaurant in the heart of Toronto's financial district.

3chefs

Michael Bonacini / Massimo Capra / Jason Parsons

OLIVER & BONACINI
RESTAURANTS

MADISON CULINARY

A Whitecap / Madison Press Book

Food photography, text, design and compilation © 2010 the Madison Press Limited
Recipes © Michael Bonacini, Massimo Capra, Jason Parsons

Published in Canada in 2010 by Whitecap Books Ltd. For more information, contact
Whitecap Books, 351 Lynn Avenue, North Vancouver, British Columbia, Canada V7J 2C4.
Visit our website at www.whitecap.ca.

The publisher acknowledges the financial support of the Government of Canada through the
Canada Book Fund (CBF) and the Province of British Columbia through the Book Publishing Tax Credit.

ISBN 978-1897330-72-2

Produced by
Madison Culinary
an imprint of
Madison Press Books
1000 Yonge Street, Suite 303
Toronto, Ontario, Canada
M4W 2K2
www.madisonpressbooks.com

Oliver & Bonacini
2433 Yonge Street
Toronto, Ontario, Canada
M4P 2E7
Phone: 416.485.8047
Toll Free: 1.888.244.6656
Fax: 416.485.7674
Email: contact@oliverbonacini.com

Garrison McArthur Photographers: photograph page v
Boston Avenue Photo Co.: photograph pages vi-vii

OGP   10 9 8 7 6 5 4 3 2 1
Printed in China

contents

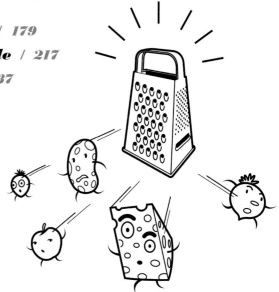

foreword

I had the pleasure of meeting the Three Chefs one at a time.

First was **Michael Bonacini**.

Michael was a guest on *CityLine* the very first time I auditioned for the show. I knew nothing! Yet he was as gracious and kind as if we had worked together for years. I immediately understood why our viewers fall for him week after week.

Michael will melt your heart and his butter at the same time. There is something very sensual about the way he walks you through a recipe, mixes a batter, and carefully plates each item.

Needless to say, our first meeting was a good one!

Next came **Massimo Capra**.

The bold, bodacious Italian chef who never skimps on full-fat flavour, Massimo is full of life, colour, and energy. His booming voice and commanding presence may lead some to believe he'd be a tough nut to crack, but I found out quickly that this magnificent chef is a big teddy bear.

Whether chopping up exotic vegetables or mixing a fragrant risotto, Massimo is a stickler for detail and design.

Oh—and that moustache! I hope he never gets rid of it.

Last, but certainly not least, came ***Jason Parsons***.

I'm not sure if it's his love of laughter or his liberal use of bacon, but Jason and I connected right away. Jason is the kind of chef you want to invite into your home. He won't get mad at you for making macaroni and cheese from a box. Just don't tell him you're using non-fat milk!

With a love of food as big as his heart, Jason is a chef worth getting to know.

The first time I hosted a Three Chefs show on *CityLine*, I was warned in advance. Our floor director told me it would be a moving train, so just sit back or get out of the way!

She was right.

Michael, Massimo, and Jason together are a recipe for extreme fun in the kitchen.

I often feel like the referee keeping score between barbs.

You'll find moments of their frivolity throughout this book, so enjoy.

And if the viewers' love for our chefs is any indication, this cookbook will be one you'll cherish for years.

Tracy Moore

1: start me up

oyster bruschetta

Oysters are one of nature's great accomplishments. For some, me included, they're too plain on their own, but top them with the right balance of flavours and wow! In this preparation, ocean meets garden—and do they ever get along. *—Jason*

serves 6

1 vine-ripened tomato, diced and
　　seeded
¼ cup/50 mL shaved Parmesan
　　cheese
½ small shallot, diced
5 basil leaves, roughly chopped
¼ garlic clove, finely chopped
12 fresh oysters
Salt and pepper

• In a bowl, mix together the diced tomato, Parmesan, shallot, basil, and garlic. Using an oyster knife, remove the top shell from each oyster. Then cut the muscle below the oyster to allow it to sit freely on the bottom shell. Place the freshly mixed bruschetta mixture on top of the oysters. Season to taste with salt and pepper. Serve immediately.

portobello mushroom chip and dip

Pile these tasty treats on a plate with a side dish of tartar sauce. For a more elegant look, spoon some tartar sauce into the bottom of a glass votive candle holder with the mushroom chips on top. *–Michael*

serves 4

for the mushrooms:
- 2 medium portobello mushroom caps, cut into finger-sized lengths
- 1 cup/250 mL all-purpose flour, seasoned with salt and pepper
- 1 egg, lightly beaten
- 1 cup/250 mL panko bread crumbs
- 1 tbsp/15 mL chopped mixed herbs (sage, thyme, chive, oregano)

for the tartar sauce:
- 1 cup/250 mL mayonnaise
- 3 small gherkins, finely chopped
- 1 shallot, finely chopped
- 2 tbsp/25 mL finely chopped parsley
- 1 tsp/5 mL lemon juice
- 1 tsp/5 mL horseradish
- 1 tsp/5 mL chopped capers
- ½ tsp/2 mL dry or Dijon mustard
- ½ tsp/2 mL chopped chives
- ½ tsp/2 mL chopped tarragon
- Salt and pepper

mushrooms: Toss the mushroom pieces in the flour. Shake off any excess, then dip the pieces first in the egg, then the panko crumbs, and finally the herb mixture. Place on a tray. Once the dipping is complete, deep fry the mushrooms in a saucepan of oil at 330° to 350°F (165° to 180°C) until golden brown and crisp. Drain on a kitchen towel.

tartar sauce: Mix all the ingredients together in a bowl and season with salt and pepper. Cover and chill. The sauce will keep for 3 to 4 days in the refrigerator.

cook's note: Substitute a seasoned mayonnaise (pesto, lemon, ginger, roasted garlic) for the tartar sauce. Button mushrooms work fine too–just provide some cocktail sticks or rosemary sprigs for dipping.

homemade honey, sage, and sea salt doughnuts

You've probably never thought to make your own doughnuts—or to serve them as a canapé. But garnishing the classic doughnut with honey and sea salt and sage creates a very interesting flavour combination and a great conversation piece. *–Jason*

makes 12 to 16 doughnuts

¼ cup/50 mL warm water
½ oz/15 g instant yeast
5 cups/1.25 L all-purpose flour
½ cup/125 mL granulated sugar
1 tsp/5 mL salt
2 eggs
1¼ cups/300 mL warm milk
⅓ cup/75 mL shortening
3 tbsp/45 mL honey
1 tbsp/15 mL sea salt
12 fresh sage leaves, chopped

- Preheat a deep fryer to 350°F (180°C).

- Mix the water and yeast in the bowl of an electric stand mixer. Let rest for 5 minutes then add 2 cups (500 mL) of the flour, plus the sugar, salt, eggs, milk, and shortening. Mix on low speed. Add the remaining 3 cups (750 mL) of flour and mix until the dough pulls away from the sides of the bowl.
- Transfer to a counter or board and knead the dough for 1 minute.
- Cover with a damp cloth and rest at room temperature until the dough doubles in size.
- Roll out the dough to about 1 inch (2.5 cm) thick; using a cookie cutter, cut it into small rings. Place the rings on a baking sheet, cover them with a damp cloth, and leave at room temperature until the doughnuts double in size.
- Deep fry immediately until golden brown. Just before serving, drizzle with the honey, sea salt, and sage.

chick pea, black olive, and pecorino crostini

Chick peas have always been a big part of my curriculum—they are the work horse of Mistura restaurant, where we've always had a variety of crostini on the menu. This version is a favourite quick giveaway on nights when we are short tables and need to make friends. *–Massimo*

makes about 24 crostini

1 baguette, cut into 24 thin slices
2 tbsp/25 mL chopped onion
2 cloves garlic, crushed
¼ cup/50 mL olive oil to sauté, plus
   more for blending
1½ cups/375 mL cooked chick peas
Salt and pepper
Juice of ½ lemon
¼ cup/50 mL Niçoise olives, pitted
   and puréed
3 oz/90 g pecorino cheese, shredded

- Grill baguette slices and set aside.
- Cook the onions and garlic in olive oil over medium heat until translucent, 2 to 3 minutes. Add the chick peas and season with salt and pepper; cook for 3 to 4 minutes, then set aside to cool.
- Pulse the chick peas and lemon juice in a blender while drizzling in olive oil to taste. You can leave it coarse or make it smooth: both ways are delicious.
- Spread some olive paste on each slice of bread and top with a spoonful of the chick pea mixture.
- Sprinkle liberally with the cheese and serve immediately.

fresh herb choux filled with lobster salad

I love travelling the east coast, where every joint has the best-ever lobster sandwich. This hors d'oeuvre is my attempt at the same effect. —Massimo

makes 16 choux

for the salad:

1 cup/250 mL lobster meat
2 tbsp/25 mL chopped celery
2 tbsp/25 mL corn kernels
2 tbsp/25 mL lemon mayonnaise
1 tsp/5 mL chopped tarragon leaves
1 tsp/5 mL chopped chives
½ tsp/2 mL grated lemon zest
½ tsp/2 mL Worcestershire sauce
Hot sauce
Salt and pepper

for the choux:

1 cup/250 mL water
¼ cup/50 mL unsalted butter
½ tsp/2 mL salt
½ tsp/2 mL granulated sugar
1 cup/250 mL all-purpose flour
1 tbsp/15 mL chopped parsley
1 tsp/5 mL chopped chives
1tsp/5 mL chopped tarragon
1 tsp/5 mL chopped thyme
4 eggs + 1 beaten egg for brushing
1 tsp/5 mL coarse sea salt
Cherry tomatoes, for garnish
Baby lettuce leaves, for garnish

- Preheat the oven to 400°F (200°C).

salad: Chop the lobster meat and mix it in a bowl with the celery, corn, mayonnaise, tarragon, chives, lemon zest, and Worcestershire. Add hot sauce, salt, and pepper to taste. Be careful not to make it too runny or the choux will be soggy.

choux: Boil the water, butter, salt, and sugar in a heavy saucepan. When the butter is melted, remove the saucepan from the heat and add the flour. Mix with a wooden spoon until it is fully incorporated. Place the mixture back on the stove on medium heat and cook for 5 to 6 minutes. The dough should be soft and come off the sides of the pot cleanly.

- Transfer to an electric mixer and use the paddle attachment at low speed to cool the dough for a few minutes. Add the fresh herbs then the eggs, one at a time, mixing thoroughly after each one is added until the dough is smooth. Check the consistency before adding the last egg. It's important that the mixture not become liquid: you want it to keep its shape, so break and whip the last egg and add it a little at a time.
- Mix the dough quickly, just until bubbles appear on the surface. Using a pastry bag (or two spoons), divide the mixture into 16 balls, about 1 inch (2.5 cm) in diameter, on a non-stick pastry sheet. Brush the tops with the egg and sprinkle with coarse sea salt. Bake for about 35 minutes or until well puffed and golden. Turn off the oven and open the door halfway to let the puffs cool slowly.
- Cut the puffs in half and fill with the lobster salad. Garnish with cherry tomatoes and baby lettuce.

maple-glazed ham, spinach, and cheese croutons

For me, this is a very versatile dish: it can be a lunchtime snack, a garnish for a salad or soup—or it can easily be transformed into a substantial sandwich. Change it up by using turkey, smoked salmon, and any kind of cheese you have on hand. —*Michael*

serves 4

12 slices ciabatta, ¼ inch/5 mm thick, or bread of your choice
Olive oil
½ shallot, finely chopped
½ clove garlic, minced
1 cup/250 mL drained and squeezed cooked spinach
2 tbsp/25 mL whipping (35%) cream
Salt and pepper
Pinch nutmeg
¼ cup/50 mL Dijon mustard
12 thin slices maple-glazed or smoked ham
⅔ cup/150 mL grated Thunder Oak Gouda cheese (Gruyère cheese or good-quality sharp cheddar can be substituted)
Cayenne pepper

- Place the ciabatta slices on a baking sheet. Drizzle them with olive oil and toast under the broiler until light golden brown. Cool.
- In a saucepan, heat a splash of olive oil over medium heat and gently cook the shallots and garlic for 2 to 3 minutes. Add the spinach and cream; season with salt, pepper, and nutmeg. Continue to cook and stir for 2 to 3 minutes, then remove from the heat.
- Spread each slice of bread with a little Dijon mustard. Top with a slice of ham, a thin layer of creamed spinach, and a sprinkling of grated cheese. Broil gently until the cheese begins to melt. Cut into ½-inch (1 cm) squares, diamonds, or triangles. Dust with a little cayenne pepper and serve.

smoked salmon and cream cheese pinwheels

I really like the flexibility of this recipe. A single pinwheel makes a great amuse bouche at the table or hors d'oeuvre at a cocktail party; several on a plate is a perfect appetizer. It also makes a terrific garnish for a plate of smoked salmon. –*Michael*

makes 24 to 30 pinwheels

for the crêpe batter:

4 eggs
½ cup/125 mL all-purpose flour
½ cup/125 mL milk
½ cup/125 mL water
½ tsp/2 mL salt
2 tbsp/25 mL melted butter
    or vegetable oil

for the pinwheels:

½ cup/125 mL soft goat cheese
¼ cup/50 mL cream cheese
3 tbsp/45 mL sour cream, plus more
    for garnish
1 tbsp/15 mL chopped dill
6 8-inch/20 cm crêpes
12 slices smoked salmon
Caviar, for garnish
Dill sprigs, for garnish

crêpes: In a medium bowl, whisk the eggs lightly. Add the flour and milk a little at a time, alternating, and whisk till smooth. Add the water and salt then whisk in the butter.

- Refrigerate for at least 1 hour.
- Lightly grease a crêpe pan with butter and heat it on medium.
- Pour approximately ¼ cup (50 mL) of the batter into the pan, tilting it and swirling the batter to cover the bottom.
- Once many bubbles have formed, loosen the edge with a spatula and flip. Cook until golden brown. (Note: the second side cooks quicker.) Slide it onto a plate and let cool.

pinwheels: In a small bowl, mix together the goat cheese, cream cheese, and sour cream to form a soft and smooth paste. Mix in the dill.

- Place six crêpes on a board and smear with the cream cheese mixture. Cover the surface evenly, leaving a ¼-inch (5 mm) edge. Place two smoked salmon slices on top.
- Roll the crêpe into a cigar shape and chill in the refrigerator for 1 hour.
- To serve, cut off the ends and slice the crêpe into four or five coins.
- Garnish with sour cream, your choice of caviar, and fresh dill.

petit brunch

Growing up in England, breakfast was always a big part of life: the pork sausage, crispy bacon, grilled tomatoes, and lots of eggs. I always thought it would be fun to capture the flavours of an English breakfast, and here you have it. The perfect canapé, breakfast in one bite! –*Jason*

makes about 28 small waffles

for the waffles:

½ cup/125 mL all-purpose flour
½ cup/125 mL buckwheat flour
4 tsp/20 mL granulated sugar
½ tsp/2 mL baking powder
½ tsp/2 mL salt
¼ tsp/1 mL baking soda
2 eggs
1 cup/250 mL buttermilk
1 tbsp/15 mL butter
1 vanilla bean

for the petit brunch:

12 arugula leaves
12 small waffles
4 strips crisp bacon
¼ cup/50 mL tomato jam
1 pork sausage, cooked
3 soft-boiled quail eggs, peeled

waffles: Preheat a waffle iron.
- Combine the flours, sugar, baking powder, salt, and baking soda.
- Whisk in the eggs, followed by the buttermilk and butter, and finally the vanilla seeds. Let the batter rest for at least 5 minutes.
- Pour a thin, even layer of the mixture on the waffle iron. Close and bake for approximately 5 minutes (depending on the waffle iron). Remove, cool, and cut into 2 x 2-inch (5 x 5cm) squares.

petit brunch: Place an arugula leaf on each waffle.
- Cut each strip of bacon into three and place a piece on each waffle, topped by a small amount of tomato jam.
- Slice the pork sausage into 12 and put one piece on each waffle.
- To finish, cut each quail egg in four and perch a piece on top of each canapé.
- Chill before serving.

cook's note: If you'd like to make your own tomato jam, Massimo's confit on page 190 would work perfectly here.

prosciutto-wrapped Gorgonzola figs

The saltiness of prosciutto is complemented by the sweetness of the figs, Gorgonzola gives a big flavour boost, and celery root lends a refreshing zest. This is a classic example of the Italian tradition that creates big flavour sensations with very simple ingredients. –*Massimo*

makes 12 pieces

3 oz/90 g Gorgonzola cheese
1 oz/30 g mascarpone cheese
¼ cup/50 mL finely shredded celery
    root
Juice of ½ lemon
Salt and pepper
6 ripe figs, cut in half
12 small slices prosciutto
¼ cup/50 mL honey
12 celery leaves

- Mix the Gorgonzola with the mascarpone in a bowl until creamy.
- Season the celery root with lemon juice, salt, and a touch of pepper. Set aside.
- Place a scoop of the cheese mixture in the middle of each fig half; top with a small amount of shredded celery root.
- Place each stuffed half on a slice of prosciutto, roll it up, and garnish it with a drizzle of honey and a celery leaf.

beef tartare crostini with poached quail eggs

Beef tartare is a popular starter in the Cremona region, in osterias and trattorias. The traditional Italian tartare is a simplified take on the celebrated French version. Since Italians don't care for the "raw" look, the lemon juice is added earlier in the process to cure the meat and brown it slightly. *–Massimo*

makes about 24 crostini

1 lb/500 g beef tenderloin, ground
Salt and pepper
1 tbsp/15 mL Dijon mustard
1 clove garlic, puréed
2 tbsp/25 mL finely chopped parsley
2 lemons
2 tbsp/25 mL olive oil, or to taste
1 baguette cut into 24 thin slices
2 tbsp/25 mL malt vinegar
24 quail eggs

- Place the meat in a bowl and season it with salt and pepper. Add the mustard, garlic, and parsley; stir well.
- Using a rasp, grate the lemons over the beef to capture all the essential oils. Stir the zest into the beef, then cut the lemons and squeeze in the juice. Add the olive oil and mix well.
- Bring a pot of salted water to a boil and add the malt vinegar. Break the eggs one at a time into a small ladle and gently place them in the water, swirling to maintain their shape. Cook for 1 to 2 minutes, or until the whites are opaque.
- Meanwhile, toast the crostini (or even better, grill them). Spoon a generous amount of beef on each slice, creating a cradle to nest one quail egg. Season with salt and serve immediately.

cook's note: The safest and tastiest strategy is to buy the tenderloin from a reputable butcher and grind it yourself immediately before preparing the tartare.

caramelized onion, goat cheese, and raisin tarts

These delicious tarts, with their sweet and savoury flavour and combination of textures, can easily be transformed into a light lunch by substituting larger tart shells. Serve with a crisp green salad. –*Michael*

serves 6

½ cup/125 mL late-harvest white wine (riesling is ideal)
¼ cup/50 mL raisins (soaked in the wine for 4 hours or overnight)
12 2-inch/5 cm tart shells
2 tbsp/25 mL olive oil
1 tsp/5 mL butter
2 onions, thinly sliced
Salt and pepper
3 tbsp/45 mL balsamic vinegar
1 tbsp/15 mL honey
¼ cup/50 mL goat cheese
Chopped chives, for garnish

- Preheat the oven to 350°F (180°C).

- Blind bake the tart shells for 6 minutes.
- Heat the olive oil and butter in a skillet over medium heat. Add the onions, season them with salt and pepper, and gently sauté for 20 to 30 minutes, until they're soft and sticky.
- Add the balsamic vinegar, honey, soaked raisins, and wine. Continue to cook for 6 to 10 minutes, then remove from the heat and cool.
- Place the tart shells on a parchment-lined baking sheet and crumble a little goat cheese into the bottom of each. Fill with the onion mixture and top with more crumbled goat cheese.
- Before serving, reheat in the oven at 325°F (160°C) for 5 to 6 minutes. Transfer to a serving platter and garnish with chopped chives.

cook's note: To blind bake the pastry, first prick it all over to prevent it from blistering and rising. Line it with parchment paper, then fill it with dried beans, clean pebbles, or pie weights. Remove the weights and paper a few minutes before the baking time is up to allow the crust to brown.

porcini mushroom and fontina cheese crêpes

At Mistura, we like to maintain a traditional feel with our creations—like this popular hors d'oeuvre. The time it takes to prepare is rewarded by the delicious flavour. In the fall, we like to hide some truffle inside, which might explain its incredible popularity. −*Massimo*

makes sixteen 3-inch (7.5 cm) crêpes

for the crêpes:

3 eggs
Pinch of salt
¼ cup/50 mL melted butter
1 cup/250 mL all-purpose flour
1¼ cups/300 mL milk

for the filling:

1 tbsp/15 mL butter
1 tbsp/15 mL oil
1 clove garlic, crushed
2 cups/500 mL fresh porcini
    mushrooms, cut in ½-inch/
    1 cm pieces
1 tsp/5 mL flour
1 cup/250 mL shredded fontina
    cheese
3 tbsp/45 mL milk
Salt and pepper
2 tbsp/25 mL chopped chives
¼ cup/50 mL cream cheese

crêpes: Crack the eggs in a bowl and stir in the salt and the butter. Mix well, then add the flour. Combine well and pour in the milk.
- Rest the batter in the refrigerator for a few hours.
- Preheat a small skillet or crêpe pan and grease it lightly. Coat the bottom with a thin layer of batter, approximately ½ oz (15 mL), and cook until set. Before it colours, turn it over and cook the other side. Repeat.

filling: Heat the butter and oil in a sauté pan. When the butter is melted, add the garlic then the porcini mushrooms. Sauté for a few minutes, then sprinkle with the flour and toss. Add the fontina, cream cheese, and milk; simmer slowly until melted completely. Season to taste and set aside.

assembly: Stir the chives into the cream cheese and set aside.
- Lay the crêpes on a towel and fill the middle of each one with the mushroom mixture. Roll into a cigar shape.
- To serve, reheat in the oven at 350°F (180°C) and serve with a garnish of cream cheese and chives.

2: soup's on

cool summer minestrone
with basil pesto and caprino cheese crostini

This is the Genovese take on an Italian classic, a version I picked up at the seaside resort hotels I worked at. It can be served hot on cooler days or at room temperature in the summer heat. *–Massimo*

serves 8

2 tbsp/25 mL olive oil
1 cup/250 mL diced onions
2 garlic cloves, chopped
8 cups/2 L vegetable stock
2 cups/500 mL diced potatoes
1 cup/250 mL diced green beans
1 cup/250 mL diced eggplant
1 cup/250 mL thinly sliced green
   zucchini
1 cup/250 mL chopped spinach leaves
Salt and pepper
1 cup/250 mL romano beans, cooked
1 baguette, sliced
7 oz/200 g fresh caprino cheese
¼ cup/50 mL basil pesto

- Heat the olive oil in a large stockpot over medium heat. Sauté the onions and garlic for 3 minutes. Add the vegetable stock and potatoes; cook for 10 minutes. Add the diced green beans, eggplant, zucchini, and spinach; season to taste. Cook for 10 minutes, then stir in the romano beans. Simmer for another 5 minutes, until the potatoes are cooked and the beans heated through. Check for seasoning.
- Toast eight baguette slices, spread them with the cheese, and set aside.
- Serve with a spoonful of pesto, a crostino, and a drizzle of olive oil.

cook's note: Caprino is an Italian goat cheese. If you can't find it, any fresh goat cheese would do. Cut all the vegetables into roughly equal pieces, starting with a ½-inch (1 cm) dice for the onions.

chilled green pea and mint soup

In England, peas and mint are a traditional pairing, so for years, while inventing myself as a chef, I would never combine the two—I always wanted to create something new. But one day, looking for a great way to capture the beauty of fresh garden peas, I had to turn to their old friend, mint. It's the ideal accent and really makes this soup sing. *–Jason*

serves 8

6 cups/1.5 L chicken stock
6 cups/1.5 L green peas
2 tbsp/25 mL chopped shallots
¼ bunch tarragon
¼ bunch mint
Salt and pepper
¼ cup/50 mL sour cream

- In a large pot, bring the chicken stock to a boil. Add the peas and return to a boil. Remove the peas with a slotted spoon and set the stock aside.
- Place the cooked peas, shallots, tarragon, mint, and half the chicken stock in a blender; purée until smooth. Slowly add the remaining stock. Season with salt and pepper then pass through a medium-fine strainer.
- Pour the soup into a bowl and place it on top of another bowl full of ice to cool it quickly. Once cool, place in the refrigerator to chill completely.
- Check the seasoning and serve with a splash of sour cream.

young carrot and riesling soup

I didn't use spices for the longest time, being afraid of overdoing them. But when I taste how the carrots come to life in this soup with just the right amount of seasoning, it makes me want to use spices more often. –*Jason*

serves 8

¼ cup/50 mL butter
1 cup/250 mL sliced shallots
2 cloves garlic, chopped
1 cardamom pod
2 cups/500 mL riesling wine
    (or other light, crisp white)
3 cups/750 mL chopped spring
    carrots
½ celery root, peeled and diced
½ cup/125 mL diced celery
½ cup/125 mL diced leeks (white only)
1 tsp/5 mL caraway seeds
5 cups/1.25 L vegetable stock
¼ bunch dill, chopped
Salt and pepper

- Melt the butter in a large pot over medium-high heat. Add the shallots, garlic, and cardamom and sauté until golden brown.
- Deglaze with 1½ cups (375 mL) of the wine, then add the carrots, celery root, celery, and leeks.
- In a separate skillet, toast the caraway seeds over medium heat until you can smell an aromatic, nutty aroma.
- Add the toasted caraway seeds to the soup along with the vegetable stock and dill.
- Bring to a simmer and cook for 25 to 30 minutes, or until the carrots are cooked through.
- Remove from the heat and purée in a blender.
- Pass through a fine strainer and return to a clean pot.
- Just before serving, add the remaining ½ cup (125 mL) of wine and season with salt and pepper.

cook's note: "Deglaze" simply means to use a liquid (in this case wine) to loosen any flavourful morsels that have stuck to the pan.

Oliver & Bonacini Café Grill mushroom soup

During my early days as a chef at the Windsor Arms Hotel, the cream of mushroom soup was far and away the most popular item on the menu. At the Oliver & Bonacini restaurants, I was inspired to create a more health-conscious version, which has since become the best-selling soup in all our restaurants to date. *–Michael*

serves 4 to 6

1 tbsp/15 mL olive oil
½ cup/125 mL chopped onions
2 cloves garlic, minced
1 sprig thyme, chopped
6 cups/1.5 L coarsely diced assorted
    mushrooms (shiitake, oyster,
    maitake, king oyster)
Salt and pepper
4 cups/1 L water
1 bay leaf
Truffle oil (optional)
1 tbsp/15 mL chopped chives
Enoki mushrooms, for garnish
Yogurt (optional)

- In a good-sized saucepan, heat the olive oil over medium heat. Gently sauté the onions, garlic, and thyme for 6 to 8 minutes without browning. Add the mushrooms to the pot a couple of handfuls at a time, seasoning with salt and pepper as you go and allowing each handful to cook down slowly. Stir constantly until all the mushrooms have been added. Pour the water over top and add the bay leaf. Simmer gently for 25 to 35 minutes, stirring occasionally.
- Purée, using a hand-held stick blender for a coarsely textured soup, or a high-speed blender for a creamy texture.
- Return to the pot and bring back to a simmer. Drizzle in a little truffle oil, if desired, and serve.
- Garnish with chives and enoki mushrooms, and if you wish, a dollop of plain yogurt.

cook's note: Almost any homemade soup tastes better the next day: there's some kind of magic that happens when it sits overnight that pulls all the flavours together, rounding them out and making them more than the sum of their parts.

slow-roasted parsnip soup with goat cheese croutons

The humble parsnip is an unfairly under-utilized vegetable. They are delicious when roasted with honey or maple syrup and turned into a coarse mash or added to scalloped potatoes. One of the easiest ways to use parsnips is in a soup such as this. –Michael

serves 4

for the croutons:
4 slices bread, toasted
½ cup/125 mL goat cheese

for the soup:
¼ cup/50 mL olive oil
1 large onion, chopped
4 cloves garlic, peeled
4 large parsnips, peeled and chopped
1 medium potato, peeled and chopped
Salt and pepper
1 sprig thyme
1 14 oz/398 mL can large white
    lima beans
4 cups/1 L vegetable stock or water
Pinch caraway seeds
¾ cup/175 mL whipping (35%) cream
Sour cream (or crème fraîche),
    for garnish
2 tbsp/25mL chopped chives

- Preheat the oven to 325°F (160°C).

croutons: Toast the bread on one side. Spread with a little goat cheese and melt under the broiler. Cut into chick pea–sized cubes.

soup: Heat the olive oil in an ovenproof sauté pan over medium heat. Sauté the onions, garlic, parsnips, and potato for 5 minutes, stirring occasionally, until softened.
- Season with salt and pepper, add a sprig of thyme, and roast in the oven for 15 to 20 minutes, until the vegetables start to turn a light golden brown.
- Remove the pan from the oven and return to the stovetop. Add the beans, stock, and caraway seeds; simmer gently for 25 to 35 minutes.
- Check and adjust the seasoning, then purée the soup in a food processor or blender.
- Return to the pan and add the cream. If the soup is too thick, add a little more broth.
- Drizzle a little olive oil on each portion then add a dollop of sour cream and a sprinkling of freshly chopped chives. Sprinkle with the croutons and serve immediately.

cook's note: This vegetarian version is terrific, but for added flavour substitute chicken stock and garnish it with smoked chicken or smoked ham hock.
- Small green lima beans are not a substitute for the large white lima beans called for here.

puréed squash and apple soup

Mistura opened for business on October 17, 1997, and this is the first soup we offered on the menu. Thirteen years later, it's still one of my favourite autumn soups: easy to make, it's delicious and popular, with the apple giving a tart and refreshing zing to balance the sweetness of the squash. —*Massimo*

serves 4

1 cup/250 mL diced butternut squash,
   1-inch/2.5 cm cubes
1 cup/250 mL diced Northern Spy
   apple, 1-inch/2.5 cm cubes
1 cup/250 mL chopped sweet white
   onions
3 cloves garlic, peeled
¼ cup/50 mL butter
Salt and white pepper
Pinch nutmeg
4 cups/1 L vegetable stock
¼ cup/50 mL sour cream, for garnish
3 tbsp/45 mL toasted pumpkin seeds,
   for garnish
1 bunch chives, finely chopped, for
   garnish

- Preheat the oven to 450°F (230°C).

- Season the squash, apples, onions, and garlic with the butter, salt, pepper, and nutmeg. Bake in the oven until soft and mushy, approximately 20 minutes.
- Purée in a blender until totally liquid, adding some of the vegetable stock if necessary.
- In a stockpot, combine the purée and the vegetable stock, and find the thickness that suits your palate. Bring to a boil and taste. Adjust for seasoning. Pass through a fine mesh strainer and set aside until needed.
- Serve with a topping of sour cream, toasted pumpkin seeds, and chives.

split pea soup

I love eating and making soups: I'll often prepare batches at home and store them in the freezer for future use. This is a hearty and simple Canadian classic: the sturdy goodness of the split peas, with their flavour rounded out by the other vegetables and the saltiness of the pork hock, makes for a meal in a bowl. Serve it with some crusty bread and a simple salad. *–Massimo*

serves 8

2 tbsp/25 mL olive oil

2 tbsp/25 mL butter

1 cup/250 mL minced onions

1 cup/250 mL minced carrots

1 cup/250 mL minced celery

2 cups/500 mL dried yellow or green
　　split peas

2 bay leaves

1 tsp/5 mL dried savoury

8 cups/2 L chicken stock

½ smoked pork hock

Salt and pepper

¼ cup/50 mL sour cream

1 bunch chives, chopped

- Heat the olive oil and butter in a heavy-bottomed pot over medium heat. Sauté the onions, carrots, and celery until they're translucent, about 5 minutes.
- Wash the split peas and drain them well, then add them to the pot along with the bay leaves and savoury. Add the stock and the pork hock and simmer gently for at least 1 hour, stirring and checking occasionally to be sure the liquid hasn't evaporated. If it seems dry, add water as needed.
- Once the peas have completely softened, remove the hock, but shred some of the meat into the soup for extra flavour. Adjust the seasoning. Mix the sour cream and chives together and add a spoonful to each bowl for garnish.

potato, fennel, and leek soup

I love this soup for the way it changes with the seasons. In the spring, the leeks and fennel are delicate and fresh, making a soup that's perfect for warm spring afternoons. In the winter, with the addition of a little whipping cream, the soup becomes a comfy blanket to warm your bones. –*Jason*

serves 8

¼ cup/50 mL butter
½ shallot, diced
3 cloves garlic, chopped
1 tbsp/15 mL fennel seed
1 star anise
1 tsp/5 mL white peppercorns
½ fennel bulb, diced
1 leek, diced
1½ stalks celery, diced
1 medium Yukon Gold potato,
    peeled and diced
½ bunch tarragon
1 cup/250 mL crisp white wine
5 cups/1.25 L chicken stock
Salt and pepper

- Melt the butter in a large pot over medium heat.
- Add the shallots, garlic, fennel seed, star anise, and white peppercorns; sauté without colouring for 1 minute.
- Add the fennel, leek, and celery and continue to sauté without colouring for another 2 minutes.
- Add the potatoes and tarragon and sauté without colour for 1 minute. Stir in the white wine and bring to a boil. Add the chicken stock and lower heat to a simmer.
- Simmer for 20 to 25 minutes, or until the vegetables are cooked through. Remove from the heat and purée in a blender. Pass through a fine strainer and season with salt and pepper.

rustic soup
with farro, cannellini beans, and black cabbage

First cultivated approximately 20,000 years ago, farro is one of the most ancient grains known to man. The main crop of the ancient Egyptians, it eventually gave way to easier-to-grow varieties of wheat. In recent years, it has enjoyed renewed popularity, emerging as a welcome variation on rice and noodles from the slow food movement in Italy. *–Massimo*

serves 8

2 cups/500 mL dried cannellini beans
2 tbsp/25 mL olive oil
1 cup/250 mL minced celery
1 cup/250 mL minced carrots
1 cup/250 mL minced onions
3 cloves garlic, minced
2 bay leaves
1 red chili pepper, chopped
1 bouquet garni with sage, thyme,
  rosemary, and tarragon
8 cups/2 L chicken stock
4 cups/1 L chopped black cabbage
2 cups/500 mL chopped tomatoes,
  peeled and seeded
2 cups/500 mL farro
Salt and pepper
Grated pecorino cheese, for garnish
Olive oil, for garnish

- Soak the cannellini beans in cold water overnight to soften them.
- Heat the olive oil in a large stockpot over medium heat. Sauté the celery, carrots, onions, and garlic until softened. Add the bay leaves, chili, and the bouquet garni; stir to blend.
- Add the stock, cabbage, tomatoes, and beans and simmer for at least 1½ hours, until the beans are cooked. Simmer very gently to prevent the beans from splitting.
- Meanwhile, cook the farro in a pot of salted, boiling water until tender. Drain and add it to the soup; simmer for a few minutes to blend the flavours.
- Season to taste with salt and pepper. Garnish with pecorino and a drizzle of good olive oil.

cook's note: Once you feel confident, cook the farro in the pot with the beans. But be careful of the timing: the high gluten content makes it easy to end up with a thicker soup than intended.

parsnip and butter bean soup

Have I mentioned how much I love the underrated parsnip? And how I think more cooks should discover their pleasures? Using parsnips in soups is the perfect way to showcase how flavourful, distinctive, and heartwarming they are. *–Michael*

serves 4

2 tbsp/25 mL olive oil
1 large onion, chopped
4 cloves garlic, chopped
2 large parsnips, chopped
3 medium potatoes, chopped
1 14 oz/398 mL can large white
    lima beans
3 cups/750 mL vegetable stock
1 bay leaf
1 tbsp/15 mL lemon juice
¼ cup/50 mL crème fraîche
2 cups/500 mL milk
Salt and pepper

- Heat the oil in a heavy saucepan over medium heat and stir in the onion and garlic.
- Cover and cook gently for 8 to 10 minutes, or until soft.
- Add the chopped parsnips and potatoes and stir well, then add the lima beans with their liquid from the can.
- Pour in the vegetable stock and add the bay leaf and lemon juice. Bring to a boil, then cover and simmer very gently for 20 to 25 minutes, or until the vegetables are completely softened.
- Discard the bay leaf and stir in the crème fraîche.
- Purée the soup in a blender in batches, thinning with the milk.
- Season and reheat before serving.
- Garnish with a few croutons.

cook's note: Two types of lima beans are commonly available: small green ones, which many people dislike, and large white ones, which are delicious. In the U.K. we call them butter beans.

ten-minute get-better chicken noodle soup

Living in Toronto, I get to meet and work with people from all over the world. One thing we all have in common is some form of chicken soup that we remember our mothers making when we were sick or feeling down. This is my quick and easy salute to all the mothers. *–Massimo*

serves 4 to 6

5 cups/1.25 L chicken broth
1 cup/250 mL minced carrots
1 cup/250 mL minced celery
1 cup/250 mL minced onions
3 cloves garlic, minced
Salt and pepper
8 oz/250 g egg tagliolini
1 cup/250 mL green peas
2 tbsp/25 mL chopped parsley
2 tbsp/25 mL chopped chives
1 tsp/5 mL butter
¼ cup/50 mL grated Parmigiano-
    Reggiano cheese

- In a large stockpot, bring the broth to a boil.
- Add the carrots, celery, onions, and garlic; simmer for 10 minutes, or until the vegetables are soft. Season to taste with salt and pepper then skim off the foam that appears on the surface.
- Crush the tagliolini with your hands and add it to the broth along with the peas. Simmer until the pasta is cooked. Remove from the heat and add the parsley, chives, butter, and Parmigiano. Mix well and serve.

oxtail and onion soup with Stilton

When I worked at the Dorchester Hotel in London, braised oxtail was a hugely popular special. Although it's time consuming to prepare, oxtail is well worth the effort, especially when used in this delicious and slightly unusual soup. Garnish it with a couple of crisp apple wedges for a clean and fresh palate cleanser. *–Michael*

serves 6 to 8

3 lbs/1.5 kg oxtail

Salt and pepper

2 tbsp/25 mL olive oil

1 carrot, chopped

2 medium onions, chopped

2 celery stalks, chopped

3 cloves garlic, sliced

1 bay leaf

1 sprig thyme

½ cup/125 mL red wine

1 cup/250 mL drained canned tomatoes

7 cups/1.75 L beef or chicken stock

1 cup/250 mL thinly sliced shiitake mushrooms

2 tbsp/25 mL red wine vinegar

1 tbsp/15 mL honey

1 tbsp/15 mL Worcestershire sauce

Stilton cheese, for garnish

- Trim the oxtail pieces and season them with salt and pepper.
- Heat 1 tbsp (15 mL) of the olive oil in a large saucepan over high heat and brown the oxtail pieces, turning occasionally, for 8 to 10 minutes. Add the carrot, half the onion, celery, garlic, bay leaf, and thyme and cook for 5 minutes.
- Add the red wine and deglaze for 2 minutes. Add the canned tomatoes and the stock. Bring to a simmer and skim the foam that appears on the surface. Be sure the oxtails remain covered with liquid. If necessary, add more broth or water. Add a little more salt and pepper and gently simmer for 2 to 2½ hours, or until the meat can be pulled away from the oxtails with ease.
- Lift out the oxtails and place them on a tray to cool.
- In a separate saucepan, sauté the remaining chopped onion in 1 tbsp (15 mL) of olive oil until soft and tender, 25 to 30 minutes. Add the shiitake mushrooms, red wine vinegar, honey, and Worcestershire sauce.
- Strain the oxtail braising liquid into the onions and gently simmer for 25 to 30 minutes. While it cooks, remove the meat from the oxtail.
- During the last 5 minutes of cooking, add the meat back to the soup. Adjust the seasoning, garnish with a crumbling of Stilton cheese, and serve with crusty bread.

mulligatawny soup

Mulligatawny comes from the Tamil people of southern India—the name means "peppery water." Based on a meat or vegetable stock generously seasoned with curry and other spices, there are many different ways this soup can be made. I've kept to a fairly traditional version. —*Michael*

serves 4 to 6

2 tbsp/25 mL butter

2 onions, peeled and chopped

Salt and pepper

¼ cup/50 mL mild curry powder
   (garam masala or madras)

2 tbsp/25 mL all-purpose flour

3 tbsp/45 mL tomato paste

1 tbsp/15 mL grated ginger

1 green apple, grated

4 cups/1 L chicken stock

1½ cups/375 mL coconut milk

⅔ cup/150 mL diced cooked chicken

¼ cup/50 mL cooked basmati rice

12 leaves cilantro, for garnish

Yogurt, for garnish

- Melt the butter in a pan over medium heat. Sweat the onions, along with salt and pepper to taste, for 3 to 4 minutes, until they begin to soften. Add the flour, curry powder, and tomato paste; cook for 2 minutes, stirring frequently.
- Turn the heat to high, and stir in the ginger and apple. Cook for approximately 3 minutes, until the apple is soft.
- Deglaze the pan with the stock. Add the coconut milk and simmer until thickened. Stir in the chicken and rice and heat through.
- Season to taste.
- Garnish with cilantro and yogurt and serve with warm naan bread.

cook's note: If you like, substitute pieces of fish or chopped cooked egg for the chicken.

early days: *Michael Bonacini*

My parents were market gardeners in Wales: potatoes, cabbage, Brussels sprouts, cauliflower, tomatoes. I remember going with my father to a small traffic island near where we lived, just a patch of green grass with three rows cut for the market. We would pull up with a truck and sell vegetables off the back.

My father originally came from Emilia-Romagna—the food capital of Northern Italy—where I've still got a lot of family. The last time I was there we had a fantastic lunch at the local Caffe Cacciatore, where my Aunt Maria was the chef for 37 years: there were 52 relatives at the table. We ate at noon and didn't leave until five o'clock!

My father had always planned to go back to Italy, but he ended up buying a piece of land near the village of Tenby, on the southwest coast of Wales. He built a guesthouse, got into farming, and then into the restaurant and hotel business. The first guesthouse was a bed and breakfast with eight rooms. We had four and a half acres of land, a little paddock up against a stream, some Welsh ponies, and some chickens for eggs. Everywhere we lived, a little garden went in with the essentials: herbs, potatoes, rhubarb, some cane fruit. I loved

working in market gardening and thought I was going to get into it myself.

My dad did the cooking at our guesthouse. He had a knack for it and could make something great out of nothing. But he never, ever made desserts. That was where my mother came in. She was born in Leicestershire and moved to Wales at age three, so she considered herself Welsh. As we were growing up, we all had to participate in the business, everything from cleaning the rooms, washing the washstand basins, ironing sheets, to peeling the potatoes in the afternoon, and doing the odd bit of room service.

I went to cooking school in the early 1970s, at Haverford-west, a small school that's still there. My sister had gone before me, which spiked my interest. I looked up to my sister and enjoyed cooking. We used to get this magazine at home called *The Caterer*, and I was always looking at the job end of things, at the hotels in London—I thought it would be great to live there. My uncle Jeffrey, who still has a hotel and catering business in South Wales, used to work at the Gros-venor House Hotel in Park Lane, and I loved to listen to his stories of various kitchens. It was fascinating. Another world.

After cooking school, I went to Italy for two weeks, then came back and started to look for work. I had decided I wanted to work in London, so I walked into the Dorchester and asked them if they had any job opportunities. They hired me as what we would call a busboy here, a commis waiter, for the sommelier. My job was running up and down stairs get-ting bottles of wine and bottles of mineral water. I had never seen so many varieties of mineral water before! Cleaning ashtrays, polishing glassware, that's what I did. It was a clas-sic place: tails for lunch, tuxedo for dinner. I remember the trancheur slicing smoked salmon, roast beef, brisket, and steak, kidney and oyster pies at the tableside.

There was a sous chef down in the kitchen who could scream like no other. His name was Nobby Clarke, and he was from Tenby! He took a liking to me, and I told him that I wanted to get into the kitchens. So he spoke to the chef, the famous Anton Mosimann.

I absolutely loved The Dorchester. I was there for almost 10 years, and I was there at the perfect time, when Mosimann had just taken over. He was a new-thinking chef; he wanted to take all that was great about the Grill Room and preserve it, but add a new spin. He wanted to put English cuisine on the map and wanted the Terrace to become a starred Michelin restaurant. Mosimann was one of the original founders of nouvelle cuisine. For ingredients we *always* had the best of the best: white asparagus, rambutans, fresh dates in clusters, fresh snails, all coming in the back door. We had a sous chef whose entire job was to manage and mature the cheeses, take care of the cheese fridges, and prepare the cheese plates. Another sous chef seasoned and preserved fruit and vegetables, season to season. A kitchen of 150 chefs, 180 bedrooms, a ratio of four employees to every guest in the hotel. It's impossible not to appreciate that. The sense of pride, the sense of teamwork, was unbelievable. Anton had a vision for each restaurant, for each part of what made up that hotel—room service, tea, bar, lounge. He knew what he wanted to do with it; he was going to make his mark, and he did. Sure enough, the Dorchester got her Michelin stars in 1984. I was proud to be a part of that.

I headed out for a year of travel in America the next year, and then came to Toronto. But I can tell you more about that next time!

3: salad days

watermelon, peach, and ginger salad with shrimp and wasabi

This is the quintessential summer salad. Very fresh, with a hint of sweetness and a surprising but welcome wasabi bite, it's perfect at lunch or for backyard entertaining. Just be sure the watermelon and peaches are ripe—you want to be able to taste the sunshine! *–Michael*

serves 4

for the dressing:

Zest and juice of 1 lime
1 thumb-sized piece of ginger, grated
1 clove garlic, minced
1 tbsp/15 mL rice vinegar
1 tbsp/15 mL wasabi powder (mixed
   with 2 tbsp/25 mL warm water)
1 tsp/5 mL soy sauce
¼ cup/50 mL olive oil

for the salad:

2 peaches, halved
1 lb/500 g large shrimp, peeled
   and deveined
1 tbsp/15 mL olive oil
Salt and pepper
8 2-inch/5 cm wedges of watermelon,
   seeds and rind removed
1 small red onion, sliced thinly in rings
1 tbsp/15 mL finely sliced mint

dressing: In a bowl, combine the lime zest and juice, ginger, garlic, rice vinegar, hydrated wasabi, and soy sauce. Whisk together.
- Slowly drizzle in the oil, whisking to emulsify the dressing. Check and adjust the seasoning.

salad: Preheat a stovetop grill pan on medium-high heat.
- Brush the peaches on both sides with oil and grill them, cut side down, until golden brown and caramelized, 3 to 4 minutes. Turn over and grill 1 to 2 minutes more. Transfer to a plate.
- Mix the shrimp with the olive oil and season with salt and pepper.
- Reheat the grill pan on medium-high heat. Cook the shrimp for 2 minutes on each side until just cooked through, then transfer them to a bowl.
- Toss half the dressing with the shrimp until the shrimp are evenly coated, and set aside. On each plate, arrange two watermelon wedges, several onion rings, and a grilled peach half. Place the shrimp around the fruit. Drizzle with the remaining dressing and sprinkle the mint over top.

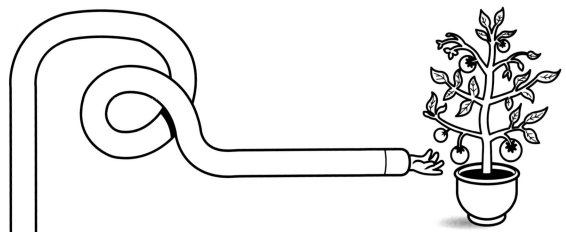

heirloom tomato carpaccio

Every time I make this dish, I am almost embarrassed by how easy it is. Then I taste it and remember how simply delicious heirloom tomatoes are when ripe. Why try to improve on perfection? Eating what's in season is truly the secret to all great recipes. *–Jason*

serves 6

6 assorted heirloom tomatoes
½ cup/125 mL goat cheese
12 basil leaves
2 tsp/10 mL sea salt
1 tsp/5 mL cracked white pepper
2 tbsp/25 mL soya bean oil

- Slice the tomatoes very thinly. Divide the slices among six large dinner plates, making a thin layer on each plate. Evenly crumble bits of goat cheese over the tomatoes and top with the freshly torn basil leaves. Sprinkle with the sea salt and cracked white pepper and drizzle with the soya bean oil.

avocado, pink grapefruit, and taggiasca olive salad

This is my spin on a salad I first had 25 years ago, in Texas, famous for its Ruby Red grapefruit. I still love eating it on a hot summer afternoon with a crisp glass of sauvignon blanc on my patio at home. It's important to serve it at room temperature to maximize the full, fresh flavours. If you like, you can add a handful of crisp bacon bits—the saltiness goes beautifully with the sweet tang of the grapefruit. *–Michael*

serves 4

for the dressing:
¼ cup/50 mL olive oil
1 tbsp/15 mL pink grapefruit juice
   (borrow a little from the segments
   for the salad)
1 tbsp/15 mL tarragon mustard
Salt and pepper

for the salad:
3 pink grapefruit
1 avocado
Lemon juice
2 heads Bibb lettuce, washed and
   left loose
¼ cup/50 mL taggiasca olives
1 handful purple basil (or regular
   basil), for garnish
¼ cup/50 mL avocado oil, for garnish
Salt and pepper

dressing: Whisk together the olive oil, grapefruit juice, and mustard. Season with salt and pepper.

salad: Peel and segment the grapefruit, squeezing the remaining pith to extract all the delicious juices. Set to one side.

- Quarter the avocado, remove the stone, and peel it. Squeeze a little lemon juice over the avocado to prevent browning. Slice the avocado into wedges and gently combine it in a bowl with the grapefruit, lettuce, olives, and dressing.

- Arrange the salad on serving plates, topping each one with several basil leaves and a drizzled tablespoon of avocado oil. Season with salt and pepper.

cook's note: Taggiasca olives come from the western part of Liguria, Italy. Used mostly for oil, they're similar to Niçoise olives, which make a suitable substitute.

baby spinach, spiced pecans, and crunchy mustard dressing

My son Oscar has instructed me never to take this popular salad off the menu. To this day, he asks the staff to hold the mushrooms and put on some extra pecans in exchange. Mom and Dad are just happy he eats his greens! *–Michael*

serves 4

for the pecans:
1 tsp/5 mL pumpkin pie spice
Pinch cayenne pepper
Pinch salt
2 tbsp/25 mL honey
½ cup/125 mL pecans

for the dressing:
¼ cup/50 mL cider vinegar
1 tbsp/15 mL honey
1 tbsp/15 mL whole-grain mustard
1 tsp/5 mL Dijon mustard
⅓ cup/75 mL olive oil
Salt and pepper

for the salad:
4 cups/1 L baby spinach
Salt and pepper
4 button mushrooms thinly sliced
4 radishes, thinly sliced
1 green apple, cut into matchsticks

pecans: Preheat the oven to 350°F (180°C). Combine the pie spice, cayenne, salt, and honey. Toss in the pecans until they're totally coated. Spread them evenly on a lined baking sheet and bake until the honey bubbles and the nuts are toasted, 10 to 15 minutes. Set aside to cool.

dressing: Combine the cider vinegar, honey, and whole-grain and Dijon mustards; whisk together. Slowly whisk in the olive oil. Season with salt and pepper and mix well.

salad: Toss the spinach with three quarters of the dressing and season with salt and pepper. Distribute the spinach on serving plates. In the same bowl, toss the mushrooms and radishes with the remaining dressing and place them around the spinach. Sprinkle the apple and pecans on top to finish.

vegetable martini

I once had a friend with a couple of fig trees in his garden. Who knew you could grow figs in Ontario, with its frigid winters? My friend had planted the trees in pots, and every winter he would wrap them up lovingly and carry them into the house. What lengths people will go to for the love of food! This fig granita is certainly worth the effort. *–Jason*

serves 6

for the tomato soup:
 5 heirloom tomatoes
 5 basil leaves
 Salt and white pepper

for the salad:
 ½ cup/125 mL diced red beets,
  cooked and peeled
 ½ cup/125 mL diced blue potatoes,
  cooked and peeled
 8 arugula leaves
 1 tsp/5 mL lemon juice
 2 tsp/10 mL olive oil
 Salt and pepper

for the fig granita:
 2 tsp/10 mL butter
 1 tsp/5 mL finely chopped shallots
 1 tsp/5 mL finely chopped ginger
 6 black figs, roughly chopped
 2 tbsp/25 mL honey
 1¼ cups/300 mL gamay noir (or any
  light, fruity red wine)
 1¼ cups/300 mL water
 1¼ cups/300 mL sugar syrup (1 part
  water boiled with 1 part sugar)
 16 lemon balm leaves, chopped

soup: Purée the tomatoes and basil leaves in a blender until smooth, then pass through a strainer to remove the seeds. Season with salt and white pepper to taste; chill.

salad: In a bowl, mix together the diced beets, potatoes, and arugula leaves. Drizzle with the lemon juice and olive oil; season with salt and pepper.

fig granita: Melt the butter in a sauté pan over medium-high heat. Sauté the figs, ginger, and shallots until the figs start to soften. Stir in the honey and wine and simmer until the liquid reduces to a third. Mix in the sugar syrup and water, then purée the mixture in a blender until smooth. Fold in the lemon balm and pour the liquid into a 9-inch (22.5 cm) square baking pan. Place the granita in the freezer until the liquid is frozen.

assembly: Fill a martini glass half-full with the chilled soup. Place some of the beet and potato salad in the centre of the glass and top with a scoop of the fig granita.

braised leek and chicken liver salad

It might not be altogether obvious, with a name like Bonacini, but I'm from Wales. So I thought it a fitting tribute to include a dish that features the humble leek, the national vegetable of Wales—proudly worn on everyone's lapel on March 1, St. David's Day. This dish can be served without the chicken livers, but once you've had it with them, you'll be hooked. *Iechyd da!* –Michael

serves 4

¼ cup/50 mL olive oil
2 tbsp/25 mL butter
1 clove garlic, minced
1 sprig thyme
4 medium-sized leeks, trimmed and
    cut into 4-inch/10 cm lengths
1 cup/250 mL chicken stock
¼ cup/50 mL tarragon vinegar
Salt and pepper
½ tsp/2 mL tarragon mustard
8 oz/250 g freshly cleaned chicken
    livers
Handful of salad greens

- Preheat the oven to 350°F (180°C).

- In a sauté pan, heat 2 tbsp (25 mL) of the olive oil and 1 tbsp (15 mL) of the butter over medium heat. Gently sauté the garlic and thyme for 2 minutes. Add the leeks and brown them lightly, about 5 minutes, turning occasionally. Add the chicken stock and half the vinegar; season well with salt and pepper. Place the pan in the oven and braise for 30 to 35 minutes, turning occasionally. Remove from the oven and cool. Most of the chicken broth should have reduced.
- Remove the leeks and place the pan on medium-high heat. Whisk in the mustard, the rest of the vinegar, a drizzle of olive oil; check the seasoning.
- In a separate pan, heat the remaining olive oil and butter. Season the chicken livers with salt and pepper and sauté until they're light golden brown, about 3 to 4 minutes.
- Place two pieces of leek in the centre of each serving plate. Add two or three chicken livers and the salad greens. Drizzle with the warm salad dressing and serve immediately.

roasted vegetables and butter leaf lettuce salad

In the dog days of summer, one of my favourite ways to eat is "al fresco." Usually the menu includes a composed salad with a great variety of roasted vegetables. With a nice helping of crusty bread, it's a meal in itself. I also use it as a side for steaks. Depending on the season, you can either roast the vegetables in the oven or do them on the barbecue. –*Massimo*

serves 4

for the dressing:
2 tbsp/25 mL finely chopped chives
2 tbsp/25 mL lemon juice
2 tbsp/25 mL olive oil
1 tbsp/25 mL Dijon mustard
1 tbsp/15 mL honey
Salt and pepper

for the salad:
8 green asparagus tips
8 white asparagus tips
4 baby green zucchini
4 baby yellow zucchini
8 baby carrots, cut in half lengthwise
1 red shepherd pepper, cut into
    ½-inch/1 cm slices
4 baby golden beets, cooked
16 French green beans
1 bunch green onions, trimmed
Olive oil
Salt and pepper
1 head butter leaf lettuce, trimmed

- Preheat the oven to 500°F (260°C).

dressing: Combine the chives, lemon juice, olive oil, Dijon mustard, honey, and salt and pepper to taste.

salad: Place the green and white asparagus tips, green and yellow zucchini, baby carrots, pepper, beets, green beans, and onions in a bowl. Toss with just enough olive oil to coat them. Season with salt and pepper and spread on a baking sheet.

- Roast in the oven for approximately 15 minutes, stirring every 5 minutes, until they've softened but are still slightly firm. Cool.

- In a bowl, gently toss the lettuce with some of the dressing, just enough to coat the leaves. Place several leaves on each plate, creating a cradle in the middle. Toss the roasted vegetables in the vinaigrette and divide among the plates.

cook's note: Shepherd peppers are extra large, sweet red peppers. If they're not available, red bell peppers are a suitable substitute.

roasted beet salad with goat cheese

I travel a lot, and one of my favourite surefire choices when dining out is a roasted beet salad. This is my interpretation of a standard, where the sweetness of the roasted beets with the tartness of the goat cheese is a match made in heaven. *—Massimo*

serves 6

12 baby beets, 4 each red, golden,
    and candy-striped
7 tbsp/90 mL olive oil
12 baby carrots
12 small red radishes
8 green onions
Salt and pepper
3 tbsp/45 mL white balsamic vinegar
3 cups/750 mL mixed baby greens
12 oz/375 g goat cheese
½ cup/125 mL toasted walnuts
2 oranges, segmented

- Preheat the oven to 400°F (200°C).

- Toss the beets with 2 tbsp (25 mL) of the olive oil and place them in a baking dish. Wrap the dish with foil and bake for 30 minutes, until the beets are tender.

- Toss the carrots and radishes with 2 tbsp (25 mL) of the olive oil and place them in a baking dish. Cook, uncovered, for 20 minutes, or until tender.

- When the beets are cooked, let them cool, then peel and halve them. Separate the colours so the red ones don't bleed into the others.

- Dress the cooked carrots and beets while still warm with some salt, pepper, and 1 tbsp (15 mL) each of olive oil and vinegar. Set aside.

- Preheat a grill pan and grill the green onions on all sides. Set aside to cool.

- Place a handful of greens on each plate and arrange a mixture of roasted vegetables on top.

- Crumble some goat cheese on each plate and sprinkle a few walnuts on top. Garnish with the green onions and the orange segments, then dress with the remaining olive oil and vinegar. Season with salt and pepper.

Burrata with arugula, eggplant, and oven-roasted tomatoes

An Italian cow's milk cheese, Burrata has become known in Canada only in the last few years. According to tradition, it was created out of a need to use up scraps of mozzarella. It is generally available only in fine food and cheese stores, but recently we've been able to find locally produced Burrata, with great results. *–Massimo*

serves 4

for the eggplant croutons:
Salt
1 lb/500 g Sicilian eggplant, cut in
   3-inch/7.5 cm sticks
1½ cups/375 mL olive oil
½ cup/125 mL all-purpose flour
2 eggs, beaten

eggplant croutons: Salt the eggplant heavily and set aside to purge for at least 30 minutes.

- In a large skillet, preheat the olive oil to 160°F (75°C) and prepare a plate with paper towels.
- Place the flour in a shallow dish. Beat the eggs in a separate bowl.
- Rinse the eggplant pieces thoroughly under water and dry. Coat them with flour, run them through the egg, then dip them in the flour again. Plunge them into the hot oil and fry until crisp, about 2 minutes per side. Set aside.

for the eggplant purée:

1 tbsp/15 mL + ½ cup/125 mL
   olive oil
1 garlic clove
2 cups/500 mL diced Sicilian eggplant
2 tbsp/25 mL water
1 tsp/5 mL grated lemon zest
Juice of 1 lemon
Salt and pepper
1 tbsp/15 mL parsley

for the tomatoes:

2 lbs/1 kg plum tomatoes, ripe but
   firm
6 tbsp/90 mL fine sea salt
¼ cup/50 mL granulated sugar
1 tbsp/15 mL rubbed thyme leaves
5 cloves garlic, thinly sliced
1 tbsp/15 mL olive oil

for the salad:

1lb/500 g Burrata cheese, split into 4
   equal portions
2 cups/500 mL arugula leaves
½ cup/125 mL pitted Moroccan black
   olives
Olive oil
Salt and pepper

eggplant purée: Heat 1 tbsp (15 mL) of the olive oil in a skillet. Sauté the garlic and diced eggplant for 1 minute then add the water. Cover and cook gently for about 4 minutes.
- Remove from the heat and place in a food processor.
- While the machine is running, add the lemon zest and juice, olive oil, and salt and pepper to taste. Transfer the purée to a bowl and set aside.

tomatoes: Preheat the oven to 250°F (120°C).
- Halve the tomatoes horizontally and remove the seeds by squeezing gently over the sink.
- Combine the salt, sugar, and thyme leaves in a bowl. Toss in the tomatoes, add the garlic and olive oil and mix well.
- Place the tomatoes cut side up on a parchment-lined baking sheet and roast for about 2 hours. Check often to be sure they don't burn.

salad: Spread some of the eggplant purée on each plate and scatter with the dried tomatoes. Place hand-broken tufts of Burrata on the tomatoes and top with the arugula and olives. Scatter some eggplant croutons around the edge and dress with olive oil and salt and pepper.

chardonnay-poached eggs on arugula salad with prosciutto and mustard dressing

I'm not a big fan of greens-only salads; I need more texture and flavour. With this salad, I love the balance of hot and cold and the warm gooeyness of the egg when you cut into it. You can substitute a grainy Dijon mustard if you don't want to make your own verjus, but I really like the softer acidity it gives to the dressing. And, of course, I love the idea of incorporating wine grapes into my recipes. *–Jason*

serves 4

for the mustard:
- 1 tsp/5 mL yellow mustard seeds
- 1 tsp/5 mL verjus (or cider vinegar)
- 2 tsp/10 mL vidal icewine (or a late harvest wine, for a cheaper option)

for the dressing:
- 1 tbsp/15 mL Dijon mustard
- 2 tsp/10 mL finely chopped shallots
- 2 tsp/10 mL finely chopped tarragon
- 2 tbsp/25 mL verjus
- 5 tbsp/65 mL grapeseed oil

for the salad:
- 2 cups/500 mL chardonnay wine (or other full-bodied white)
- 4 eggs
- 4 cups/1 L baby arugula
- 4 cups/1 L organic watercress
- 1 cup/250 mL shaved Parmesan cheese
- 12 slices prosciutto
- White pepper

mustard: Grind the mustard seeds with the verjus. Stir in the icewine and chill.

dressing: Whisk together the mustard, shallots, and tarragon. Slowly add the verjus followed by the grapeseed oil.

salad: Heat the wine in a small pot over medium heat until almost boiling. Crack the eggs into individual cups. Gently drop them into the liquid, ensuring the eggs are covered with liquid while they poach. Adjust the heat if necessary to maintain a simmer. Poach for 2 to 5 minutes, until the eggs are soft to the touch. Remove with a slotted spoon and dry on a paper towel.

- In a salad bowl, mix the arugula, watercress, shaved Parmesan, and mustard dressing to taste.
- Layer the salad and prosciutto on four plates and top with a warm poached egg. Season the egg with a sprinkle of white pepper and serve.

cook's note: Verjus is a sour liquid made from unripe grapes. You can squeeze your own or look for it in specialty food stores.

lobster Caesar salad

A few years ago, on an east coast trip, my wife and I stopped at a simple restaurant whose menu was overrun by lobster. We had lobster Caesar and lobster pizza. Over the next few days, we worked our way through lobster bisque, butter-poached lobster, lobster rolls, and so on. When I came home, I had to create my own version of lobster Caesar salad. *–Jason*

serves 4

for the dressing:
2 egg yolks
4 tsp/20 mL verjus (or cider vinegar)
1 clove roasted garlic, crushed
1 anchovy
1 tsp/5 mL Dijon mustard
Dash lemon juice
Dash Worcestershire sauce
½ cup/125 mL olive oil
4 tsp/20 mL water
2 tbsp/25 mL grapeseed oil
2 tbsp/25 mL grated Parmesan cheese
Salt and pepper to taste

for the croutons:
1 cup/250 mL diced sourdough bread
1 tbsp/15 mL oil from the roasted garlic
1 tbsp/15 mL chopped rosemary
Salt and pepper

for the salad:
3 heads romaine lettuce
½ cup/125 mL dressing
2 cups/500 mL lobster meat
1 cup sourdough croutons
2 cups/500 mL shaved Parmesan cheese

· Preheat the oven to 400°F (200°C).

dressing: Combine the egg yolks, verjus, garlic, anchovy, mustard, lemon juice, and Worcestershire together in a blender. Slowly add in the olive oil, followed by the water, and finally the grapeseed oil. Blend thoroughly, then add the Parmesan and season with salt and pepper.

croutons: Mix together the bread, garlic oil, and rosemary. Spread on a baking sheet and toast in the oven until golden brown, about 5 to 7 minutes. Toss occasionally to ensure even toasting. Drain on paper towels, season with salt and pepper, and cool.

salad: Wash the romaine in very cold water and drain on paper towels. Remove the outer leaves, leaving only the sweet, crisp hearts. Trim half an inch (1 cm) from the top and bottom of the heart and discard. Cut the hearts in half and place them in a large bowl. Drizzle with the Caesar dressing to taste and toss. Add the lobster meat, garlic croutons, and shaved Parmesan and serve.

cook's note: To roast garlic, simply cut the top off a whole head, drizzle it with about ¼ cup (50 mL) of olive oil, sprinkle it with sea salt, and roast it in a 325°F (160°C) oven for approximately 45 minutes.

Asian-style coleslaw and Peking duck salad

For a chef, taking a trip to the local Chinatown is a fascinating and wondrous way to spend a few hours. You can eat well and inexpensively and be inspired by a great culture that has been very influential on North American eating habits. Bringing home a Peking duck and turning it into a salad such as this is a tasty memento of a day spent in Chinatown. *–Michael*

serves 4

for the dressing:
- 3 tbsp/45 mL fish sauce
- 3 tbsp/45 mL lime juice
- 2 tbsp/25 mL brown sugar
- 2 tbsp/25 mL vegetable oil
- 1 tbsp/15 mL soy sauce
- 1 Thai chili, thinly sliced

for salad:
- ½ head napa cabbage
- 1 green mango, peeled and sliced
- 1 cup/250 mL bean sprouts
- 1 carrot, peeled and shredded
- ½ cup/125 mL snow peas, thinly sliced
- Meat of ½ Peking duck, removed from bone and sliced into strips
- ½ cup/125 mL coarsely torn mint, cilantro, and Thai basil leaves
- ¼ cup/50 mL chopped toasted peanuts
- 1 green onion, sliced on the diagonal
- 4 sprigs cilantro, for garnish
- 4 wedges lime, for garnish

dressing: In a bowl, whisk together the fish sauce, lime juice, brown sugar, vegetable oil, soy sauce, and chili in a bowl.

salad: Toss the cabbage, mango, bean sprouts, carrots, and snow peas together in a large bowl. Stir in the duck, herbs, peanuts, and green onions.
- Drizzle the dressing over top and toss well.
- Garnish with cilantro leaves and a wedge of lime.

cook's note: Peking (i.e. Beijing) duck originated hundreds of years ago. Key to the dish is the crispiness of the skin, which is achieved by basting the bird with a hot, sweet liquid then leaving it to dry before cooking.

spring greens and chanterelles with soft-boiled egg

Each year, restless from cooking the same items all winter long, my cooks and I anxiously await the arrival of the spring "primizie," the first produce of the season. We get a jump on these products by flying them in from the west coast, but as soon as the weather turns, we look for the Ontario foragers who sell us the fruit of their painstaking work. This salad is one of my favourites and often appears on the spring menu. *–Massimo*

serves 4

1 cup/250 mL fresh fiddleheads,
    washed and trimmed
1 bunch green asparagus tips,
    3 inches/7.5 cm long
1 bunch white asparagus tips,
    3 inches/7.5 cm long
3 tbsp/45 mL olive oil
⅓ cup/75 mL bacon, cut in ¼-inch/
    5 mm cubes
4 whole ramps (wild leeks), coarsely
    chopped
1 cup/250 mL small chanterelle
    mushrooms
Salt and pepper
3 tbsp/45 mL sherry vinegar
1 head Boston lettuce, torn into bite-
    sized pieces
1 head frisée lettuce, torn into bite-
    sized pieces
4 soft-boiled eggs (cooked 3 minutes)

- Cook the fiddleheads and green and white asparagus tips in boiling water for 1 minute. Blanch them in ice cold water and set aside.
- Heat 2 tbsp (25 mL) of the oil in a skillet over medium heat. Sauté the bacon for 3 minutes, then add the ramps and mushrooms. Season with salt and pepper; cook until the ramps are soft, approximately 4 minutes. Add 2 tbsp (25 mL) of the vinegar to the skillet and let it evaporate, then remove from the heat. Add the cooked vegetables and toss until warm.
- Mix together the Boston and frisée lettuces and divide them equally among plates. Arrange equal amounts of vegetables over the lettuce and season with salt and pepper. Drizzle the remaining sherry vinegar and olive oil over top. Just before serving, break an egg over the middle of each salad.

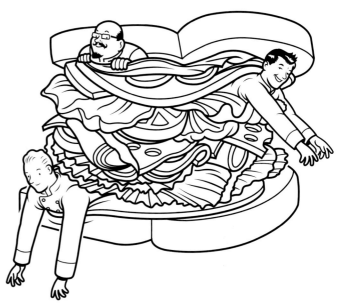

4: let's do brunch

Tuscan villa frittata

Last year a group of us travelled through Italy, with a stopover in Tuscany. Our villa had a perfectly equipped kitchen, its own vegetable garden—and egg-laying chickens. One morning I gathered fresh eggs from the chicken pen and vegetables from the garden, and added pancetta and cheese we'd bought in the market. Being in that early-morning kitchen, allowing the region's ingredients to write their own recipe, is one of my most memorable moments as a chef. *–Jason*

serves 6 to 8

1 tbsp/15 mL butter
1 cup/250 mL sliced pancetta
1 tbsp/15 mL sliced shallots
1 tsp/5 mL chopped garlic
½ cup/125 mL sliced mushrooms
1 cup/250 mL sliced zucchini
1 cup/250 mL chopped asparagus
½ cup/125 mL diced tomato
2 tbsp/25 mL chopped fennel ferns
    (or fresh dill)
1 tbsp/15 mL grapeseed oil
8 fresh farm eggs, where available
½ cup/125 mL half-and-half (10%)
    cream
Salt and pepper
¾ cup/175 mL grated Parmesan
    cheese
¼ cup/50 mL pecorino cheese
    (or mozzarella)

- Preheat the oven to 400°F (200°C).

- Melt the butter in a non-stick pan over medium heat. Stir in the pancetta, shallots, garlic, and then the mushrooms. Sauté without allowing to colour for 2 minutes (if they do, just add a little water to slow things down), then add the zucchini, asparagus, and tomato. Continue to sauté without colour for another 2 minutes.
- Remove from the heat and add the fennel ferns. (If you're not making your frittata right away, chill the vegetables.)
- Heat the oil in a wide cast-iron pan over medium-high heat.
- Whisk the eggs and cream and season with salt and pepper. Add to the hot pan and stir with a wooden spoon. Once the eggs start to come together, stop stirring and add the sautéed vegetables. Transfer the frittata to the oven and bake for 5 to 8 minutes.
- Mix the Parmesan with the pecorino and sprinkle over the frittata. Bake for another 5 minutes, then remove and let sit for 2 minutes before serving.

omelette Arnold Bennett

This dish, which makes an elaborate and delicious breakfast, lunch, or dinner, was created especially for the novelist Arnold Bennett by the chef of the Savoy Hotel on The Strand, in London, England. I was greatly impressed by the size of the kitchen on my first visit to the Savoy back in 1978—it was the biggest I'd ever seen and even still had a coal-fired stove! *–Michael*

serves 2

for the sauce:
- 1¼ cups/300 mL whipping (35%) cream
- 6 oz/175 g smoked haddock fillets, boneless, skinless, diced into walnut-sized pieces
- ½ cup/125 mL grated cheese of your choice (cheddar, Gruyère, Parmesan), plus more for finishing
- Salt and pepper
- 1 tsp/5 mL finely chopped chives
- ¼ tsp/1 mL dry mustard

for the omelette:
- 1 tsp/5 mL butter
- 5 eggs, beaten
- Salt and pepper
- 2 tbsp/25 mL whipping (35%) cream

sauce: In a small saucepan over medium heat, bring the cream to a simmer, add the haddock, and cook gently for 3 to 4 minutes. Remove the haddock from the cream and increase the heat to medium-high. Reduce the cream by approximately one quarter, then turn the heat down to medium and stir in the cheese. Season with salt and pepper and stir in the chives and mustard. The sauce should be thick enough to coat the back of a spoon. Reduce further, if necessary. When the sauce is the right consistency, add back the haddock and keep it warm.

omelette: Heat the butter in a non-stick pan over medium heat. Season the beaten eggs with salt and pepper; stir in the cream. Pour the eggs into the pan and prepare a simple, flat omelette.

- Place on a warm serving plate and spoon the cheese and haddock sauce over top. Sprinkle with a little extra cheese and broil lightly before serving.

mushroom and spinach gratin
with peameal bacon and scrambled eggs

Add a grilled portobello mushroom or a char-grilled tomato, seasoned simply with thyme and sea salt, for a delicious and welcoming brunch or breakfast. This is just the right balance of comfort and richness. *–Michael*

serves 4

3 tsp/15 mL butter

2 cups/500 mL sliced button mushrooms

Salt and pepper

4 handfuls spinach, washed

3 tbsp/45 mL + ¼ cup/50 mL whipping (35%) cream

Pinch nutmeg

8 slices peameal bacon

¼ cup/50 mL grated Parmesan cheese

8 eggs

¼ cup/50 mL milk

- Heat 1 tsp (5 mL) of the butter in a sauté pan over medium-high heat. Sauté the sliced mushrooms, seasoning lightly with salt and pepper, for 2 to 3 minutes. Add the spinach and cook down, allowing the moisture to evaporate. Add 3 tbsp (45 mL) of the cream and season with salt, pepper, and nutmeg.
- Grill or pan-fry the peameal bacon. Place two to three slices on each plate and add a mound of spinach and mushrooms in the centre. Sprinkle with a generous helping of Parmesan cheese and place under a preheated broiler until the cheese turns a light golden brown. Turn the broiler off and keep the gratin hot in the oven.
- In a small, non-stick skillet, melt 2 tsp (10 mL) of the butter over medium heat.
- Beat the eggs and stir in the milk. Gently scramble by stirring the eggs from the outside edges of the pan to the centre. When the eggs are soft, tender, and almost cooked, adjust the seasoning, add the rest of the cream, and remove them from the heat. Adding the cream is the trick to perfect scrambled eggs, as it adds a layer of richness and stops the eggs from cooking further and becoming hard and dry.
- Spoon over the top of the spinach and mushroom gratin and serve.

oeufs à la coque
with asparagus, bacon, and buttered toast

This is a simple-to-make dish, and it's one of my favourite ways to eat eggs. In my family, the longstanding tradition was to have eggs this way, "with His soldiers," that is, the asparagus, bacon, and buttered toast, the day after Easter, as part of the celebration of renewal. I still remember my mother busy cutting bread and boiling more eggs while my father, brothers, and I worked through what she'd already cooked. —*Massimo*

serves 4

8 eggs, at room temperature
8 slices bacon, cooked crisp
4 slices bread, toasted and buttered
8 green asparagus spears, steamed
8 white asparagus spears, steamed
Salt and pepper

- Fill a pan large and deep enough to hold all the eggs with enough water to just cover them, and bring to a boil. Using a slotted spoon, gently place each egg in the water. Boil for at least 2½ minutes then remove. Serve immediately with bacon, buttered toast (if you like, cut it into strips for easier dipping), asparagus, and salt and pepper to taste.

peameal bacon and fried eggs
with crispy onions and potato and tomato salad

I did not grow up eating bacon and eggs for breakfast: for me a cappuccino and a fresh baked brioche is all it takes to get going in the morning, and eggs are normally served at dinner. When I arrived in this part of the world, I was taken to a diner for breakfast and learned about Canadian-style breakfast—and peameal bacon. At first I thought it was strange to call it bacon, but I quickly grew accustomed to its good qualities, mainly its big flavour and relative lack of fat. –*Massimo*

serves 4

for the onions:
- 2 cups/500 mL thinly sliced sweet white onions
- 1 cup/250 mL buttermilk
- 2 cups/500 mL vegetable oil
- 3 tbsp/45 mL cornstarch
- Salt

onions: Soak the onions in the buttermilk for at least 4 hours. Heat the oil in a large pot to 150°F (70°C). Drain the onions and toss them in the cornstarch.

- Fry the onions, stirring gently until they start to turn golden. Remove them from the oil with a slotted spoon and drain them on paper towels. Season to taste with salt.

for the potatoes:

2 cups/500 mL diced baking potatoes

2 tbsp/25 mL olive oil

2 tbsp/25 mL butter

1 sprig rosemary

1 sprig thyme

1 sprig sage

2 cloves garlic, sliced

Salt and pepper

for the tomatoes:

16 cherry tomatoes

1 tsp/5 mL salt

1 tsp/5 mL pepper

1 tsp/5 mL thyme leaves

1 tsp/5 mL granulated sugar

1 tbsp/15 mL olive oil

for the assembly:

1 head frisée lettuce, washed

Salt and pepper

1 tsp/5 mL red wine vinegar

¼ cup/50 mL olive oil

1 cup/250 mL roasted potatoes

1 cup/250 mL crispy onions

2 tbsp/25 mL butter

8 slices peameal bacon

4 eggs

potatoes: Bring a pot of salted water to boil and cook the potatoes for 5 minutes, until half cooked. Drain and cool.
- Heat the oil and butter in a skillet over medium-high heat and sauté the potatoes until they're brown on all sides. Once the potatoes start to colour, add the rosemary, thyme, sage, and garlic. When the potatoes are crispy, remove them from the heat and drain the excess fat. Season with salt and pepper and set aside.

tomatoes: Preheat the oven to 150°F (70°C). Cut the cherry tomatoes in half and dress with the salt, pepper, thyme, sugar, and oil. Spread them on a wire rack and roast them in the oven until they're dehydrated, about 2 hours. Set aside.

assembly: Place the frisée in a bowl. Add the roasted tomatoes and season with salt and pepper. Toss with the vinegar and half the oil, then add the potatoes. Divide the salad among four plates and sprinkle the crispy onions on top. Heat half the butter and the remaining oil in a skillet over medium heat and fry the bacon until it's golden on both sides. Place two slices of bacon on each plate. In the same skillet, melt the remaining butter and fry the eggs, one at a time. Place the eggs on the bacon and serve immediately.

smoked salmon, goat cheese, and asparagus quiche

The secret to great quiche is using lots of filling. Don't try to economize by cutting back—you'll just end up with a lumpy custard tart. –Jason

makes two 8-inch (20 cm) tarts

for the pastry:
- 3 cups/750 mL cake and pastry flour
- 1¼ cups/300 mL shortening
- 2 tbsp/25 mL brown sugar
- 1 tbsp/15 mL salt
- ⅔ cup/150 mL cold water

for the filling:
- 3 eggs
- 2 cups/500 mL half-and-half (10%) cream
- 2 cups/500 mL milk
- ¼ tsp/1 mL grated horseradish
- Salt and white pepper
- 1 tsp/5 mL butter
- ¼ cup/50 mL sliced shallots
- ½ tsp/2 mL finely chopped garlic
- 1 cup/250 mL roughly chopped smoked salmon
- 1 cup/250 mL chopped asparagus, blanched
- ½ cup/125 mL chopped fennel, blanched
- 2 tbsp/25 mL roughly chopped dill
- Salt and pepper
- ½ cup/125 mL goat cheese

- Preheat the oven to 450°F (230°C).

pastry: Place the flour in a large bowl and crumble in the shortening.
- In a separate bowl, dissolve the sugar and salt into the water. Slowly mix the water solution into the flour to form a soft dough. Cover with plastic wrap and chill in the refrigerator for at least 45 minutes. Roll out the chilled dough to ¼ inch (5 mm) thick, line two 8-inch (20 cm) quiche pans, and chill again for at least 15 minutes.
- Blind bake the quiche shells for 6 to 8 minutes to set the crust. To do this, prick the pastry all over so it doesn't blister or rise. Line it with parchment paper, then fill it with dried beans or pie weights. Remove the weights and paper a few minutes before the end of the baking time to let the crust brown. Take out of the oven, remove the weights and paper, and cool.
- Reduce the oven to 350°F (180°C).

- **filling:** Whisk the eggs, then add the cream, milk, and horseradish. Season to taste with salt and white pepper.
- Melt the butter in a skillet over medium heat. Add the shallots and garlic and sauté until golden brown. Remove from the heat and add the smoked salmon, asparagus, fennel, and dill. Mix well and season with salt and pepper.
- Place the filling in the quiche shells, layering in the goat cheese. Pour the quiche mixture over the filling and bake in the oven for 45 minutes to 1 hour, until the mixture is just set. Remove from the oven and cool for 15 minutes.

quick and easy hollandaise

This simple sauce is excellent with freshly cooked asparagus, poached eggs (like those on the next page) or fish, or grilled beef tenderloin. It must be used immediately though—it will hold together only for an hour or so, and it must be kept warm. —*Michael*

makes approximately 1 cup/250 mL

1 cup/250 mL butter
2 egg yolks
4 tsp/20 mL warm water
Juice of ¼ lemon
1 tbsp/15 mL tarragon vinegar
Salt and white pepper
Pinch cayenne pepper

- Clarify the butter by warming it in a small saucepan over gentle heat. Once the butter has melted completely, remove the pan from the heat and let it stand for 15 minutes to allow the solids to separate. Gently drain off the clarified butter, keeping it warm and close at hand.
- Place the egg yolks, half the warm water, the lemon juice, and vinegar in a bowl. Whisk vigorously over a saucepan of hot water until the yolks are thick and creamy—it should take 3 to 4 minutes. Slowly whisk in the clarified butter, a little at a time. Season with salt, pepper, and a touch of cayenne.
- If the hollandaise is too thick, add a little more warm water. If it's too thin, add a little more clarified butter.

poached eggs
with Swiss chard, bacon, chorizo, and hollandaise

I'm a creature of habit, and this is one of my favourite treats on weekends. It's a great brunch dish for anyone (like me) who prefers breakfast to be on the savoury—rather than sweet—side. Although the ingredients are fairly simple, I love the complexity of flavours and textures involved. –*Michael*

serves 2

1 tbsp/15 mL butter

1 cup/250 mL diced bacon,
  ½-inch/1 cm chunks

1 cup/250 mL diced chorizo sausage

½ small onion, diced

½ clove garlic, minced

1 bunch Swiss chard, stems and
  centre ribs cut out and chopped,
  leaves coarsely chopped

Salt and pepper

2 tbsp/25 mL malt vinegar

4 eggs

1 cup/250 mL hollandaise (see recipe
  on preceding page)

1 tsp/5 mL chopped chives

Pinch smoked paprika

- Heat the butter in a sauté pan over medium-high heat.
- Gently sauté the bacon and chorizo until the bacon is crisp and the sausage is golden brown. Remove from the pan and drain some of the excess oil.
- Turn heat to low and cook the onions and garlic for 2 to 3 minutes.
- Add the Swiss chard stems and cook for 5 minutes, stirring occasionally. Add the leaves and season with salt and pepper. Continue cooking and stirring for 8 to 10 minutes.
- Add back the bacon and chorizo. Cover the pot, turn off the heat, and let sit.
- In a separate pot of boiling, salted water, add the malt vinegar and poach the eggs gently for 3 minutes.
- Divide the chard mixture between two plates and perch two poached eggs on top.
- Spoon the hollandaise over the eggs; sprinkle with chives and smoked paprika.

cook's note: I like to use apple-smoked bacon, but any good-quality bacon will do.

scallop Benedict

Taking a classic and making it my own is one of my favourite things to do as a chef. Eggs Benedict is a great dish because of the complexity of flavours, but when you change the egg to a scallop, the bacon to prosciutto, and the muffin to a scone, it just gets that much better. –Jason

serves 4

for the cheddar scones:
- 2¾ cups/675 mL all-purpose flour
- ⅓ cup/75 mL granulated sugar
- 4 tsp/20 mL baking powder
- 1 tsp/5 mL salt
- 1¼ cups/300 mL shortening
- 1 cup/250 mL shredded aged cheddar cheese
- ⅔ cup/150 mL + 2 tbsp/25 mL buttermilk

for the hollandaise:
- 2 egg yolks
- ¼ cup/50 mL riesling wine (or other light, crisp white)
- Zest and juice of ½ lemon
- 1 cup/250 mL clarified butter
- Salt and pepper

- Preheat the oven to 400°F (200°C).

- **scones:** In a large bowl, mix together the flour, sugar, baking powder, and salt.
- Cut in the shortening to create a crumble, then mix in the cheese and ⅔ cup (150 mL) of the buttermilk. Gather the soft dough into a ball, wrap in plastic wrap, and chill until firm.
- Roll out the dough to 1 inch (2.5 cm) thick. Cut into squares and place evenly on a baking sheet. Brush the top of the scones with the remaining buttermilk and bake for 12 to 15 minutes.
- Cool on a wire rack.

- **hollandaise:** Place the egg yolks, wine, lemon zest, and juice in a stainless-steel bowl. Place the bowl over boiling water and whisk vigorously. The eggs will cook slowly while incorporating air bubbles. Once you can form a figure eight on the top of the egg mixture that holds to the count of eight, start to add the clarified butter very slowly. Pour a constant stream of butter into the eggs while continuing to mix.
- Once all the butter has been added, season with salt and pepper.
- Keep the hollandaise warm until ready to use.

for the Benedict:

6 cheddar scones, cut in half

12 slices prosciutto

12 baby arugula leaves

2 tsp/10 mL grapeseed oil

12 large scallops

Benedict: Preheat the oven to 375°F (190°C).

- Lay 12 scone bottoms on a large baking tray and top each with a slice of prosciutto and a leaf of arugula.
- Heat the oil in a large skillet over high heat, add the scallops, and sear both sides until golden brown.
- Place one scallop on each scone and warm through in the oven (approximately 2 to 3 minutes).
- Top each with a spoonful of hollandaise and serve three scone halves per person.

cook's note: To clarify butter, warm it in a small saucepan over gentle heat. When it's melted, remove the pan from the heat and let it stand for 15 minutes to allow the solids to separate. Skim any foam off the surface and pour off the clear butter.

- The scone recipe will give you 10 to 12 scones. Refrigerate or freeze what's left—they make great snacks.

lobster, leek, and potato pithiviers

A pithivier (named after a town in France) can be anything sandwiched between two rounds of puff pastry. Although I love them, I don't often put them on the menu because they don't present that well in a restaurant, where all the plates have to be little shows: all the ingredients are beautiful and delicious, but they're hidden away in the pastry. They're perfect for home, though, and with puff pastry widely available, the possibilities are endless. *–Jason*

makes 8 pithiviers

1 tsp/5 mL butter
1½ cups/375 mL diced leeks
½ cup/125 mL sliced shallots
¼ cup/50 mL diced bacon
1 cup/250 mL diced cooked potato
½ cup/125 mL whipping (35%) cream
1 tsp/5 mL Dijon mustard
1 cup/250 mL lobster meat
¼ cup/50 mL triple-cream Brie cheese
12 leaves fresh basil, torn
Salt and pepper
4 3-inch/7.5 cm rounds puff pastry
2 egg yolks, beaten
4 5-inch/12.5 cm rounds puff pastry

- Preheat the oven to 350°F (180°C).

- Melt the butter in a skillet over medium heat. Sauté the leeks, shallots, and bacon for 2 minutes without allowing to colour.
- Add the potatoes, cream, and mustard; simmer until the cream reduces by half. Remove from the heat and add the lobster, Brie and basil; season with salt and pepper.
- Place in the refrigerator. When cool, lay the small puff pastry rounds on the counter.
- Using a pastry brush, coat the pastry with egg yolk.
- Place a generous portion of the lobster, leek, and potato filling in the centre of the pastry, leaving a ½-inch (1 cm) ring around the edge. Top with the large pastry rounds.
- Using your thumb and finger, pinch around the edge to seal the pithivier. Brush the outside with more egg yolk and put the pastry in the refrigerator.
- Once chilled, bake the pithiviers in the oven for 12 to 15 minutes, until golden brown.
- Remove from the oven and cool for 2 minutes before serving.

crêpes with prosciutto cotto, fontina, asparagus, and truffle

I must confess that this is not my recipe—it is actually one of my mother's and it's one of her best. Every time I go to visit her, she makes it for me and my family. It is part of her modern, fancy repertoire, a recipe she learned after I started cooking. –Massimo

makes 12 crêpes

for the béchamel:
¼ cup/50 mL butter
⅓ cup/75 mL all-purpose flour
1½ cups/375 mL milk
1 cup/250 mL grated Asiago cheese

for the crêpes:
3 eggs
Pinch salt
¼ cup/50 mL melted butter
1 cup/250 mL all-purpose flour
1¼ cups/300 mL milk

béchamel: Melt the butter with the flour in a saucepan over medium heat, mixing well, until it takes on a light golden colour. Remove from the heat and cool for a minute. In a separate pan, bring the milk to a boil, then add it to the butter and flour, stirring well to prevent lumps. Return to a boil, lower heat, and simmer for 20 minutes. Remove from the heat and add the Asiago. Mix well and set aside.

crêpes: Crack the eggs in a bowl and add the salt and the butter. Mix well, then add the flour. Mix well and add the milk. Rest the batter in the refrigerator for a few hours.

- Lightly grease a 7-inch (17.5 cm) skillet and preheat it to medium. Coat the bottom with a thin layer of batter. Before it colours, turn it over and cook the other side.

for the filling:

24 small spears green asparagus, peeled and cooked

12 spears white asparagus, peeled and cooked

1 tbsp/15 mL butter

Salt and pepper

½ oz/15 g black truffle

12 6-inch/15 cm crêpes

2 cups/500 mL béchamel sauce

12 slices fontina cheese

8 slices prosciutto cotto (Italian ham)

1 cup/250 mL grated Grana Padano cheese

for the sauce:

¼ cup/50 mL butter

2 shallots, peeled and finely chopped

¼ cup/50 mL vegetable stock

1 cup/250 mL whipping (35%) cream

¼ cup/50 mL grated Grana Padano cheese

for the garnish:

2 bunches thin asparagus

2 tbsp/25 mL butter

Salt and pepper

½ oz/15 g black truffle

filling: Preheat the oven to 375°F (190°C).

- Cut the asparagus into 2-inch (5 cm) pieces.
- Heat the butter in a skillet, then add the asparagus and season with salt and pepper. Shave in the truffle, sauté for 1 minute, and set aside.
- Lay the crêpes out flat and spread a thin layer of béchamel on each one. On top place a slice of fontina, a slice of ham, two spears of green asparagus, and one white. Sprinkle on some Grana Padano, then roll the crêpe into a cannelloni shape.
- Arrange the filled crêpes in a buttered ovenproof dish and bake until hot and slightly crispy, about 5 minutes.

sauce: Heat the butter in a sauté pan over medium heat and sauté the shallots for 3 minutes, until tender. Add the vegetable stock and cream and adjust for seasoning, if necessary. Cook for approximately 2 minutes, until creamy looking. Remove from the element, add the Grana Padano, and whisk until it's incorporated. Set aside and keep warm.

garnish: Blanch the asparagus in salted, boiling water for about 4 minutes. Drain and cool in ice water and set aside.

- Heat the butter in a skillet over medium-high heat, add the asparagus, and season with salt and pepper. Shave in the truffle and sauté for 3 minutes. Set aside and keep warm.

assembly: Spread some sauce on the bottom of each plate, lay the crêpe on top, and garnish with the sautéed asparagus. Shave a little Grana Padano on top and serve at once.

cook's note: Grana Padano is a hard, aged cheese with a granular texture that's suited to grating. It's less salty than Parmigiano and more delicate in flavour, so if you substitute with Parmigiano, just use a little less.

smoked salmon on rye
with bacon and asparagus tartar sauce

This sandwich starts with a straightforward classic: smoked salmon on rye bread. The tartar sauce gives it a fun twist and the possibilities are endless. You can play with the ingredients, adding chunky bits of whatever vegetable you like that's available. *–Jason*

serves 4

for the tartar sauce:
¼ cup/50 mL chopped asparagus, blanched
1 tbsp/15 mL chopped capers
1 tbsp/15 mL chopped gherkins
1 tbsp/15 mL chopped tarragon
½ cup/125 mL mayonnaise
1 tbsp/15 mL lemon juice

for the sandwich:
8 slices dark rye bread
12 slices smoked salmon
2 shallots, thinly sliced
12 slices bacon, cooked crisp
2 heirloom tomatoes, thinly sliced
1 cup/250 mL arugula

tartar sauce: Combine the asparagus, capers, gherkins, and tarragon. Fold in the mayonnaise and lemon juice and set aside.

sandwich: Toast the rye bread and spread some tartar sauce on four of the slices. Pile on the smoked salmon, shallots, bacon, tomatoes, and arugula, then top with the remaining slices of toasted bread.

my Canadian sandwich

As a teenager, my friends and I spent a lot of time in the pool halls and arcades of Cremona. The owner of our favourite spot was a young man who had recently returned from a backpacking trip to America with some great and strange ideas about food: burgers and hot sandwiches with steak and bacon and eggs, and all of it cooked on a griddle. The older folks were sure he was doomed to fail, but we thought he was onto something. *–Massimo*

serves 4

for the caramelized onions:
2 tbsp/25 mL butter
1 tbsp/15 mL olive oil
2 cups/500 mL sliced onions
Salt and pepper

onions: Heat the butter and oil in a skillet over medium heat. When the butter has melted, add the onions. Season with some salt and pepper and simmer gently, stirring occasionally, until the onions are caramelized and start to brown.

for the sandwich:
4 ciabatta buns or padas
¼ cup/50 mL tomato sauce
8 slices Gruyère cheese
¼ cup/50 mL caramelized onions
8 strips bacon, cooked crisp
24 oz/750 g cooked roast beef
Salt and pepper
1 tsp/5 mL thyme leaves

sandwich: Cut the buns in half and spread some tomato sauce on each half. On each bottom half, layer a slice of Gruyère followed by some caramelized onions, two strips of bacon, and a quarter of the beef. Season with salt, pepper, and thyme then finish it off with one more slice of cheese and the top of the bun. Grill in a panini press until the cheese is melted.

grilled salmon croque monsieur

This is comfort food at its best. When we started serving brunch a year and a half ago, we thought it would be a good idea to include smoked salmon, which is how this sandwich started. From there it evolved to grilled salmon with great cheese, horseradish, and really good French bread: basically, all the things I like to eat. *—Jason*

serves 8

3 lbs/1.5 kg salmon fillet
2 tsp/10 mL grapeseed oil
2 baguettes
¼ cup/50 mL grape mustard
2 cups/500 mL baby arugula
8 slices triple-cream Brie cheese
6 eggs
1 cup/250 mL half-and-half (10%)
   cream
1 tsp/5 mL grated fresh horseradish
¼ cup/50 mL butter
Icing sugar for dusting

- To cut the salmon, turn your knife on a 45-degree angle to the fillet and slice down on the diagonal. This should give you approximately 16 slices ¾ inch (2 cm) thick, about 3 oz (90 g) each.
- Rub the salmon with the grapeseed oil and place it on a hot grill. Mark the salmon for about 1 minute on each side and remove it from the grill.
- Cut the baguette into 16 slices. Spread the grape mustard on eight slices and top with the baby arugula. Place the grilled salmon over that then finish with a slice of Brie and a slice of baguette.
- In a bowl, mix the eggs, cream, and horseradish. Dip the sandwiches in the egg mixture, coating both top and bottom.
- Heat the butter in a skillet over medium-high heat and fry the sandwich until golden brown on both sides. Finish by warming it in the oven just enough to soften the Brie, dust it with icing sugar, and serve.

pulled duck club sandwich

While filming *Spoons and Suitcases* in Charleston, South Carolina, I met a star chef named Sean Brock. Sean took me and the crew to the local watering hole to pound back some beers and grab some chow after the gig. One offering was a duck club sandwich so good I decided it would be a crime not to try to reproduce it. We had a lot of fun that night, but here is what I remember—or at least my interpretation of it. —*Massimo*

serves 4

for the pulled duck:

1 cup/250 mL diced red pepper
1 cup/250 mL diced onions
4 cloves garlic, crushed
1 sprig rosemary
1 sprig sage
1 sprig thyme
1 tbsp/15 mL chopped parsley
1 tbsp/15 mL chopped chives
1 tsp/5 mL granulated sugar
½ tsp/2 mL salt
4 duck legs
2 tbsp/25 mL olive oil
2 tbsp/25 mL butter
1 cup/250 mL drained canned
    tomatoes
¾ cup/175 mL beer, preferably dark
    ale
½ cup/125 mL chicken stock
Salt and pepper

duck: Preheat the oven to 300°F (150°C).

- In a large bowl mix the peppers, onions, garlic, rosemary, sage, thyme, parsley, chives, sugar, and salt. Toss in the duck legs to distribute the seasoning. Wrap with plastic wrap and let rest in the refrigerator for at least 3 hours.
- Heat the oil and butter in a saucepan over medium heat. Add the onions, peppers, and herbs from the marinade and sauté for 3 minutes, until translucent. Add the tomatoes and cook until the juices evaporate. Add the duck legs and sprinkle them with the beer. Set alight to burn off the alcohol, then add the chicken stock. Cover and roast in the oven for 1½ hours, or until the leg bones move easily.
- Cool to room temperature.
- Remove the duck, reserve the vegetables, and discard the herbs.
- Pull the meat from the bones and discard the skin. Add the duck meat to the vegetables, check the seasoning, and reheat without burning.

for the chipotle mayonnaise:

¼ cup/50 mL mayonnaise

2 tbsp/25 mL puréed chipotle peppers

2 tbsp/25 mL finely chopped red
onions

1 tsp/5 mL honey

for the caramelized onions:

2 cups/500 mL thinly sliced onions

1 tbsp/15 mL oil

2 tbsp/25 mL butter

Salt and pepper

for the iceberg slaw:

½ head iceberg lettuce, shredded

¼ cup/50 mL shredded red onions

¼ cup/50 mL thinly sliced sweet
gherkins

½ cup/125 mL shredded carrots

2 green onions, thinly sliced

2 tbsp/25 mL mayonnaise

for the sandwich:

12 slices of bread

¼ cup/50 mL chipotle mayonnaise

8 slices bacon, cooked crisp

4 large tomato slices

mayonnaise: Combine all the ingredients and set aside.

onions: Heat the oil and butter in a skillet over medium-low heat. Add the onions, season with some salt and pepper, and simmer gently, stirring occasionally, until the onions start to brown and caramelize.

slaw: In a bowl, mix the lettuce with the onions, gherkins, carrots, and green onions. Add the mayonnaise and mix well.

sandwich: Spread each slice of bread with mayonnaise. On four slices, pile some of the pulled duck, a layer of slaw, and a slice of tomato. Top with another slice of bread followed by more duck, more slaw, and two slices of bacon. Cap it all off with the last four slices of bread. You might want to skewer the sandwiches with cocktail sticks to hold them together.

Aunt Lina's torta di mascarpone croque monsieur

This sandwich is close to my heart in many ways: my Aunt Lina often made this for me when I visited her. She managed a wealthy landowner's house and lived in a large mansion with maids and nannies. To an eight-year-old farmboy, that old house was a marvel, and this sandwich was the icing on the cake. The torta di mascarpone is the secret dimension, somehow managing to be delicate and rich at the same time. –*Massimo*

serves 4

for the béchamel:
¼ cup/50 mL butter
⅓ cup/75 mL white flour
1½ cups/375 mL milk
1 cup/250 mL grated Grana Padano cheese

for the croque monsieur:
¼ cup/50 mL butter
8 slices sandwich bread
8 slices Gruyère cheese, ⅛ inch/2.5 mm thick
12 oz/375 g ham, sliced thin
¼ cup/50 mL béchamel sauce
4 tsp/20 mL torta di mascarpone
2 tbsp/25 mL grated Parmigiano-Reggiano cheese

béchamel: Melt the butter with the flour in a saucepan over medium heat, mixing well, until it takes on a light golden colour. Remove from the heat and cool for a minute. In a separate pan, bring the milk to a boil, then add it to the butter and flour, stirring well to prevent lumps. Return to a boil and cook for 20 minutes. Remove from the heat and add the cheese. Mix well and set aside.

- Preheat the oven to 375°F (190°C).

croque monsieur: Spread the butter on four slices of the bread and set aside.
- On each of the unbuttered slices, place a slice of Gruyère, a quarter of the ham, another slice of Gruyère, and a buttered slice of bread.
- Mix together the béchamel and torta di mascarpone.
- Place the sandwiches on a baking tray and drizzle them with the béchamel mixture. Bake until the topping is melted and slightly golden. Remove from the oven, sprinkle with the Parmigiano, and serve immediately.

cook's note: If you can't find torta di mascarpone, fold together equal parts of Gorgonzola and mascarpone cheese.

zucchini, Gouda, and walnut soufflé

Despite a traumatic experience in England in my early days as a chef, I love making and eating cheese soufflés. Although many people are intimidated by the idea, they're actually quite manageable for any home cook. You can easily make them ahead and chill them, then reheat them for a very impressive dish. *–Jason*

serves 4

2 tbsp/25 mL butter, softened
3 tbsp/45 mL ground bread crumbs
3 tbsp/45 mL ground toasted walnuts
¼ cup/50 mL butter, softened
¼ cup/50 mL all-purpose flour
¾ cup/175 mL milk
3 eggs, separated
¼ cup/50 mL grated Gouda cheese
1 tsp/5 mL lemon juice
¾ cup/175 mL grated zucchini,
   blanched
Salt and pepper

- Preheat the oven to 350°F (180°C).

- Rub the butter around the inside of five 4 oz (125 mL) ramekins.
- Combine the bread crumbs with the ground walnuts and sprinkle them inside the ramekins so they stick to the butter. Set aside.
- Melt the butter in a pan over medium-high heat, then add the flour and whisk until smooth. Cook for 2 minutes, then add the milk in three equal parts, whisking smooth after each addition. Remove from the heat and add the egg yolks, then the grated Gouda.
- In a bowl, whisk the egg white with the lemon juice until they form stiff peaks. Fold them into the cheese mixture, add the zucchini, and season with salt and pepper.
- Fill the prepared ramekins to the top.
- Place the soufflés in a water bath and bake for 30 to 35 minutes. They're done when a toothpick comes out almost, but not perfectly, dry. Remove the ramekins from the water, let them cool, then remove the soufflés from the ramekins and chill them in the refrigerator.
- To serve, reheat them in a 400°F (200°C) oven for 8 minutes.

Saint-Honoré cheese, apricot, and truffle honey tart

Saint-Honoré cheese from Quebec is the Cadillac of Brie: so rich and creamy and so packed with flavour, especially when it's warm and gooey. Increasingly popular, you should be able to find it at fine cheese shops. Combined with the sweet/savoury blend of apricot and rosemary, it's sophisticated and comforting at the same time. *–Jason*

serves 4

for the tart:

1 sheet puff pastry
4 apricots, halved
2 tbsp/25 mL chopped rosemary
1½ tbsp/22 mL truffle honey (or any flavourful honey)
4 slices Saint-Honoré cheese, ½ inch/1 cm thick

for the apple salad:

1 apple, thinly sliced
2 cups/500 mL arugula
½ cup/125 mL toasted walnut halves
2 tbsp/25 mL soya bean oil
1 tbsp/15 mL lemon juice
Salt and pepper

- Preheat the oven to 400°F (200°C).

tart: Divide the puff pastry into four rectangles (4 x 2 inch/10 x 5 cm).
- Slice the apricots into small wedges and lay them across the puff pastry. Sprinkle with the rosemary and bake in the oven for 7 minutes. Drizzle with the truffle honey and continue to bake for 2 minutes, or until the pastry is light golden brown.
- Remove the tarts from the oven, top with a slice of Saint-Honoré, and allow the warmth of the pastry to soften the cheese.

apple salad: Combine the apple with the arugula, walnuts, soya bean oil, and lemon juice. Season with salt and pepper and serve it with the warm tart.

cook's note: Puff pastry is available in grocery stores. Try to find a product that uses butter and as few stabilizers as possible. If you can't find pre-rolled sheets, roll the dough out to ¼ inch (5 mm).

early days: *Massimo Capra*

My connection with food has always been very large. I grew up on a farm near Cremona, and we raised and grew everything that we ate. It was a big farm, about 3,000 acres, and my parents were agricultural workers. I remember my father being in the garden picking carrots, radishes, tomatoes, peppers—you name it; he would sit there on a little stool in the garden, wash and rinse them in fresh water, a bit of salt. He would have a bun in one hand, a little bowl for dipping in olive oil in the other, and eat the fresh-picked vegetables. The food was all around us.

My father passed away a few years ago at 93 (I was born when he was 50). After the war he spent about 10 years being the boss, but he never wanted to have anything to do with anything but his farm animals; he just wanted to maintain the way of life he had before the war. He was *really* a family man; family was very important to him. He used to eat the fat and he would give me the good parts of the meat.

My mother cooked a lot. She's over 80 now, and she still makes pasta by hand. It was a totally different way of life. When I was three or four my mother would clean a chicken and give me the raw liver to eat, because they believed that

was a good thing. I loved it! I would be right there—me and the cat!

Everything I ate until I went away to cooking school was raised or grown in and around our village. With the exception of when my older brother went away to join the army; when he moved to Genoa he was meeting comrades from Sicily, from Calabria, from all over. He would bring salami and wine, and they would bring their specialties, like really good olive oil, and trade. So when I was eight, we started getting some really good things from all over Italy.

I used to cook for the neighbours for free when I was young. Our neighbour Carla worked all day, doing piecework for Benetton. So I would go over and make spaghetti with tomato sauce. Just as a tease, everybody would ask me to cook for them.

My parents never asked me to be anything other than what I wanted to be. "We can only recommend, but it's up to you; you have to pick your own path." There was one chef in my town, and he travelled the world, and my mother was always keen on travel. I was good at painting and drawing, and in Italy they guide you toward a career, so they always were guiding me towards the arts—but I had to go work, simple as that. I decided I had to choose a cooking school. That would get me away from the village, would get me money quickly, and food was something I really understood and enjoyed being around.

To earn some money the summer before starting cooking school, I worked on a farm near home. I was working in one of those cherry pickers, picking the tops off corn. I was 13 years old, it was 1973, and it was a job that paid an *enormous* amount of money, $30 a day! I was the only kid in the cherry picker with eight cages—me and seven older ladies. My very first day on the job it was extremely hot, there was a storm coming, and the job needed to be completed. We worked from eight in the morning until nine at night, and I *fainted* in the cherry picker, I was so tired! I couldn't finish. There was an older lady, she must have been in her 60s, she was picking her tops and she was picking mine, because I just keeled over. Unbelievable! I did it for a month, seven days a week straight. I made the equivalent of $900 and gave the money to my parents for tuition and to rent my apartment.

My first year at school, at Salsomaggiore in Parma, I boarded; but I was bored, and the extra cost was a burden on my parents. So the next year I got a train pass and commuted—and then the school always placed me in different hotels, which I liked, even though we had to do a lot of menial work. Everything was very professional. At some places I was treated like a galley slave, and at others I was treated very well. My first year, at Tratorria Dall'Amelia in Venice, I took six months of abuse, only to be told at the end of the year they liked me and wanted me to come back.

I came to Canada in February 1984, in the middle of a huge snowstorm. I arrived with the 25-cent piece my uncle had given me two years earlier so I could call him when I arrived in Toronto to work at his restaurants. I took a cab to his restaurant on St. Clair Avenue West and picked my way through giant snow banks to the curb and his door. It was here that I learned the importance of Italian cuisine and *la cucina nuova* to other people. But that is the beginning of another story!

5: nice catch

scallop gratin Trattoria dell'Amelia

I have always been lucky in my employment, starting with my very first job at the Trattoria dell'Amelia, just outside Venice, when I was 15. One of my early tasks was cleaning two 50-kilogram bags of fresh scallops first thing in the morning, which I'm sure was a kind of hazing. It was an amazing experience, however, and this recipe for the most popular preparation of those scallops has stayed with me ever since. *–Massimo*

serves 4

¼ cup/50 mL butter

¼ cup/50 mL lemon juice

2 tbsp/25 mL brandy

1 tbsp/15 mL dry mustard

Salt and pepper

2 tbsp/25 mL olive oil

1 cup/250 mL diced crusty Italian bread

3 cloves garlic, minced

2 tbsp/25 mL chopped parsley

1 tbsp/15 mL grated Grana Padano cheese

16 large scallops and their shells (can be purchased separately)

- Preheat the oven to 450°F (230°C).

- Prepare the sauce by blending the butter, lemon juice, brandy, and mustard. Season with salt and pepper and set aside.
- Heat the oil in a skillet over medium heat. Add the bread and garlic and toast until the bread is crispy and golden. Remove from the heat and toss in the parsley and cheese, then set aside.
- Place a scallop on each shell and arrange the shells on a baking sheet. Drizzle some of the sauce over each scallop and bake for 8 to 10 minutes.
- Remove from the oven, sprinkle each scallop with bread, and serve immediately with a light salad on the side.

cook's note: If Grana Padano is not available, substitute Parmigiano-Reggiano or aged Asiago.

scallop, goat cheese, and cherry tomato tart

This is a really popular summer dish and I often have it on the lunch menu. It's light, fresh, and simple, but the flavours are so satisfying. –Jason

serves 4

for the pesto:
1 cup/250 mL basil leaves
¼ cup/50 mL olive oil
1 clove garlic, crushed
1 tsp/5 mL salt
½ tsp/2 mL pepper

for the tart:
1 sheet puff pastry
16 red cherry tomatoes
16 yellow cherry tomatoes
1 cup/250 mL goat cheese
¼ cup/50 mL basil leaves
16 large scallops
1 tbsp/15 mL grapeseed oil
Salt and pepper

• Preheat the oven to 400°F (200°C).

pesto: Place the basil leaves, olive oil, garlic, salt, and pepper in a blender. Purée until smooth.

tart: Roll the puff pastry to about ⅛ inch (2.5 mm) thick. Cut the pastry into four circles using a 4-inch (10 cm) cookie cutter. Pierce well with a fork to prevent the pastry from rising too much, and lightly brush it with pesto. Cut the cherry tomatoes in half and place them on the puff pastry rounds. Bake for 10 to 12 minutes, until the pastry is golden brown. Remove from the oven and sprinkle with goat cheese and basil leaves. Brush the scallops with the oil and grill them for 2 minutes on each side. Season with salt and pepper, and serve four on each tart.

conger eel stewed in white wine, onions, and tomato

The Po River cuts across northern Italy from the west to the east and has many tasty gifts to offer, including conger eels. My uncles were all fishermen, some of them professional. At the end of eel season we used to gather the family and have a great party with fried smelts, stewed eel, handmade pasta, and sauce by the riverside fishing barrack. Eel, with its rich, sweet, firm meat, has been a sentimental favourite ever since. *–Massimo*

serves 4

¼ cup/50 mL olive oil

2 lbs/1 kg conger eel, filleted

2 cups/500 mL thinly sliced white
   onions

4 cloves garlic, sliced

2 red chili peppers

1 tsp/5 mL dried oregano

1 cup/250 mL white wine

1½ cups/375 mL chopped, peeled,
   and seeded plum tomatoes

½ cup/125 mL pitted Gaeta olives
   (or substitute kalamata)

Salt and pepper

- Heat half the oil in a skillet over medium-high heat. Sear the fillets on both sides until golden. Remove from the pan and keep warm.
- Add the remaining oil to the skillet and sauté the onions, garlic, chilis, and oregano until translucent. Stir in the wine and let it evaporate, then add the tomatoes. Simmer for 5 minutes on high heat, then return the eel to the pan. Add the olives, reduce the heat to medium, season to taste with salt and pepper, and simmer gently until cooked, about 10 minutes.

signature lobster linguini

I call this "my signature" because it represents a kind of turning point I hit a few years ago. As a young chef, trying to prove myself, I often would over-complicate things. But with this dish, I decided to find something simple and do it really well, using good, fresh ingredients. I haven't been able to take it off the menu since—if I try, I get too many complaints. Matched to the wine you use in the preparation—something rich, creamy, and refreshing—it's a beautiful and simple pleasure. *–Jason*

serves 4

for the black truffle pasta:
¾ cup/175 mL all-purpose flour
¾ cup/175 mL semolina flour
1 egg
3 egg yolks
1 tbsp/15 mL truffle paste
Olive oil
Water

for the linguini:
1 tbsp/15 mL butter
½ cup/125 mL chopped bacon
¼ cup/50 mL sliced shallots
¼ cup/50 mL chardonnay wine
   (or other full-bodied white)
½ cup/125 mL whipping cream
4 cups/1 L fresh black truffle linguini
1 cup/250 mL chopped lobster meat
¼ cup/50 mL basil leaves
½ cup/125 mL shaved Parmesan
   cheese
Salt and pepper
Dash truffle oil

pasta: Mix the two flours together. Slowly add the whole egg, followed by the egg yolks, and finally the black truffle paste. Knead the mixture together: if it's too dry, add a dash of olive oil and water. It is better for the dough to be slightly moist than too dry. Wrap with plastic wrap and place in the refrigerator to firm up. Use a pasta machine to roll out portions of the chilled linguini.

linguini: Melt the butter in a skillet over medium-high heat. Add the bacon and shallots and sauté for 2 minutes. Add the wine and reduce by half, followed by the cream.

- Cook the linguini in boiling water. Drain the pasta and add it to the bacon and shallot mixture, followed by the lobster, basil, and half the Parmesan.
- Season with salt and pepper and serve. Garnish with a drizzle of truffle oil and the remaining cheese.

butter fried trout with all things green

You can prepare this dish with just about any green vegetable, depending on the season. If they're firm or dense, you'll have to blanch them, but leafy greens like spinach, sorrel, and arugula can just be tossed into the pan—they'll cook quickly. Your timing must be careful though: the acidity from the wine and lemon juice will quickly turn the vegetables grey, so speed is essential. I like to serve the fish on the bone, for maximum flavour and moisture. *–Michael*

serves 4

4 cups chopped green summer vegetables (asparagus, green peas, fava beans, edamame, fiddleheads, escarole, spinach), cut into equal-sized pieces
¼ cup/50 mL butter
8 trout fillets, cleaned and trimmed
¼ cup/50 mL white wine
¼ cup/50 mL vegetable stock
¼ cup/50 mL whipping (35%) cream
¼ cup/50 mL mixed fresh herbs (tarragon, parsley, chervil)
Salt and pepper
Juice of ½ lemon

- Blanch the firmer vegetables (fiddleheads, asparagus, etc) in boiling salted water; refresh in a bowl of ice water. Drain well and set aside.
- Heat 3 tbsp (45 mL) of the butter in a good-sized non-stick pan over medium-high heat. Fry the fillets skin-side down for 3 to 4 minutes. Remove from the pan and keep warm.
- In the same pan, add the blanched vegetables and greens. Stir in the wine, stock, and cream; simmer for 2 minutes. Add the herbs, stir in the remaining butter, and season to taste with salt and pepper. Squeeze in the lemon juice and spoon the mixture into four serving bowls.
- Place the fillets on top and serve immediately.

whipped salt cod, grilled polenta,
and dandelion salad

Salt cod is one of my favourite fish dishes, and it's very easy to prepare once the salt
has been removed by soaking. With many recipes dedicated to it throughout southern
Europe, it is securely lodged in my cultural background. Whipping salt cod is a popular
preparation in both Nimes, France, and Vicenza, Italy; I've taken the liberty of combining
the two traditions to maximize the result and minimize the fuss. I've even added a little
green to make it that much healthier. –*Massimo*

serves 4

for the cod:

1 lb/500 g salt cod

1 medium potato, diced

2 cloves garlic

Salt

1 cup/250 mL milk

½ cup/125 mL olive oil

3 tbsp/45 mL lemon juice

Pepper

for the polenta:

8 cups/2 L water

¼ tsp/1 mL salt

1 tbsp/15 mL olive oil

1 lb/500 g yellow cornmeal, medium
  ground

1 tbsp/15 mL butter

4 oz/125 g grated Parmigiano-
  Reggiano cheese

½ cup/125 mL chopped mixed herbs
  (parsley, chives, basil)

for the dandelion salad:

1 bunch tender dandelion greens,
  tough stems removed, shredded

2 tbsp/25 mL olive oil

1 clove garlic, sliced

3 tbsp/45 mL chopped red onions

4 anchovies, chopped

1 tbsp/15 mL white wine vinegar

Salt and pepper

cod: Soak the cod in fresh water for a couple of days, changing the water often.

- Cook the potato in boiling water with the garlic cloves and salt until the potatoes are tender. Drain the potatoes, then add the milk and cod to the pot and simmer gently for 3 minutes. Remove the pot from the stove and drain.
- Place the cod and potatoes in a food processor and purée, adding olive oil until the mixture is smooth. Add the lemon juice and salt and pepper to taste.

polenta: Bring the water to a boil, season with the salt and oil, and reduce the heat to low. Whisk in the polenta in a gentle cascade. Once it's all added, stir constantly with a wooden spoon for 45 to 50 minutes.

- When it's cooked, whisk in the butter, Parmigiano, and chopped herbs and turn it out in a baking dish to cool. Cut into even slices and grill them in a greased grill pan.

salad: Place the shredded dandelions in a bowl.

- Heat the olive oil in a skillet over medium heat and add the garlic, onions, and anchovies. Cook until the anchovies dissolve, then sprinkle in the vinegar. Let it evaporate for a few seconds, then quickly pour the mixture over the dandelions. Toss with salt and pepper, and serve it with the polenta and salt cod.

perch "saltimbocca" with strawberry, white asparagus, and green pea salad

I first learned about and fell in love with veal saltimbocca when I was working in Bermuda. I still think that's funny: surrounded by fish and I remember sage leaves and prosciutto sandwiched between two pieces of veal escalope. It wasn't until I came back to Niagara and discovered delicate Lake Erie perch that I thought to put fish and saltimbocca together. *–Jason*

serves 4

for the perch:
8 large sage leaves
8 perch fillets
8 thin slices bacon
1 tbsp/15 mL grapeseed oil
Salt and pepper

for the salad:
1 cup/250 mL fresh local strawberries
1 cup/250 mL 2-inch/5 cm pieces white asparagus spears, blanched
1 cup/250 mL fresh green peas
1 tbsp/15 mL roughly chopped mint leaves
2 tbsp/25 mL soya bean oil
Salt and pepper

perch: Place one sage leaf on the skin side of each perch fillet. Wrap a slice of bacon around the centre of each fillet to hold the sage in place. Heat the grapeseed oil in a skillet over high heat. Sear the fish for approximately 1 minute on each side, skin side first. Season with salt and pepper.

salad: Toss together the strawberries, white asparagus, peas, mint, oil, salt, and black pepper. Serve with the seared perch.

pistachio crusted swordfish
with eggplant purée, fennel, and raisins

About 22 years ago, I worked for Michael Carlevale at Prego della Piazza. This is a recipe I developed there, based on the famous swordfish involtini of Sicily. I still find it very fresh and interesting—and easy to prepare. —Massimo

serves 4

for the eggplant purée:

½ cup/125 mL olive oil
1 clove garlic, crushed
2 cups/500 mL diced Sicilian eggplant
2 tbsp/25 mL water
Zest and juice of 1 lemon
Salt and pepper
1 tbsp/15 mL parsley

for the swordfish:

4 6 oz/180 g swordfish steaks
Salt and pepper
2 cups/500 mL raw pistachios, ground
   to the coarseness of sea salt
¼ cup/50 mL olive oil
2 fennel bulbs, cut in wedges
3 tbsp/45 mL raisins
1 tsp/5 mL granulated sugar
2 tbsp/25 mL vinegar
2 shallots, thinly sliced
¼ cup/50 mL white wine
¼ cup/50 mL orange juice
1 tsp/5 mL Dijon mustard
1 cup/250 mL eggplant purée

- Preheat the oven to 450°F (230°C).

purée: Heat 2 tbsp (25 mL) of the olive oil in a skillet over medium heat. Sauté the garlic and eggplant for 1 minute. Add the water, cover, and cook gently for about 4 minutes.
- Transfer to a food processor. While it's running, add the lemon zest and juice, the remaining olive oil, and salt and pepper to taste. Remove and set aside.

swordfish: Season the swordfish with salt and pepper; coat the top and bottom with the ground pistachios. Bake in the oven for approximately 8 minutes.
- At the same time, heat 1 tbsp (15 mL) of olive oil in a sauté pan over medium heat. Add the fennel, raisins, sugar, and salt to season; cook for 5 minutes. Add the vinegar and let evaporate completely. Set aside.
- Meanwhile, heat another 1 tbsp (15 mL) of olive oil in a skillet over medium heat and cook the shallots until softened. Add the wine and let it evaporate, then pour in the orange juice and reduce by two thirds. Transfer the liquid to a deep bowl. With a stick blender, blend in 1 tbsp (15 mL) of olive oil and the mustard to emulsify. Add a few drops of lemon juice, if needed, to make it tart. Season with salt and pepper and set aside.
- Spread some eggplant purée on each plate, along with some fennel and raisins, and place the swordfish on top. Drizzle the vinaigrette around and over the fish to serve.

pan-fried red snapper
with artichoke, mushroom, and black olive ragoût

This recipe calls for snapper, but you can use just about any fish available. The ragoût also goes well with seared scallops and meat dishes like veal scaloppine or pork noisettes. That is the essence of cooking—taking a recipe and changing it up to make it your own. Don't be afraid to experiment and play with the ingredients! –*Michael*

serves 4

2 tbsp/25 mL butter

4 6 oz/180 g red snapper fillets, cleaned and deboned

Salt and pepper

3 tbsp/45 mL olive oil

2 shallots, finely diced

1 clove garlic, minced

2½ cups/625 mL sliced mixed mushrooms (button, oyster, king oyster, shiitake)

¼ cup/50 mL white wine

½ cup/125 mL quartered and drained canned artichoke bottoms

3 ripe plum tomatoes, diced

½ cup/125 mL pitted black olives

¼ cup/50 mL chicken stock

4 lemon wedges, for garnish

4 tsp/20 mL chopped parsley

- Heat 1 tbsp (15 mL) of butter in a good-sized sauté pan over medium-high heat. Lightly season the snapper with salt and pepper and fry skin-side down for 3 to 4 minutes. Turn, add the remaining butter, and cook for 2 to 3 minutes longer. Remove from the pan and cover with foil to keep the fish hot.
- Using the same pan, add the olive oil and quickly sauté the shallots and garlic for 1 to 2 minutes. Add the mushrooms and cook for 3 to 4 minutes. Stir in the white wine and simmer for 1 minute. Stir in the artichokes, tomatoes, olives, and chicken stock. Season with salt and pepper and simmer, stirring occasionally, for 2 to 3 minutes.
- Spoon the ragoût onto four plates and place a fillet on each. Garnish with lemon, chopped parsley, and a drizzle of oil.

steamed halibut and preserved lemon with fall vegetable tagine

I love the flavours and spices of north Africa. I was first introduced to them some years ago, on a trip to Tunisia. Later, in England, I shared an apartment with a Moroccan guy my sister was dating. He loved to cook, but, worried about the smells, he'd line the bottom of the door with towels so the other tenants wouldn't be bothered. I, however, loved the floral aroma that would linger for days afterward and still find ways to work those incredible spice mixtures into my own cooking. *–Michael*

serves 4

for the preserved lemons:
12 lemons, washed
Juice of 6 lemons
Coarse kosher salt

for the dukkah:
½ cup/125 mL hazelnuts
¼ cup/50 mL coriander seeds
3 tbsp/45 mL sesame seeds
2 tbsp/25 mL cumin seeds
1 tsp/5 mL fennel seeds
1 tbsp/15 mL black peppercorns
1 tsp/5 mL dried mint leaves
1 tsp/5 mL salt

preserved lemons: Quarter the lemons, leaving enough uncut at the bottom that they remain intact. Sprinkle the inside of each lemon with about 1 tbsp (15 mL) of kosher salt, then reshape the fruit.

- Place 3 tbsp (45 mL) of kosher salt in the bottom of a Mason jar. Layer the lemons with salt in between until the jar is three quarters full. Add enough lemon juice to almost fill the jar, then seal it. Store at room temperature for about a month, flipping it upside down every few days. The lemons are ready when the rinds are soft. Rinse the lemons before using.

dukkah: In a heavy skillet over high heat, dry toast the hazelnuts for 3 to 4 minutes, until slightly browned and fragrant, being careful not to burn them. Remove from the heat and cool completely. Repeat with the coriander, sesame, cumin, and fennel seeds, and the peppercorns. Allow them to cool completely.

- Place the nuts, seeds, mint, and salt in a mortar. Pound until the mixture is crushed, or pulse in a food processor to a coarse consistency. Do not allow the mixture to become a paste.

for the fish and tagine:

2 tbsp/25 mL olive oil

2 onions, diced

2 carrots, diced

6 small potatoes, skin on, cut in half

1 cup/250 mL diced butternut squash

1 tbsp/15 mL grated ginger

1 clove garlic, minced

1½ tsp/7 mL ground coriander

½ tsp/2 mL ground turmeric

½ tsp/2 mL ground cumin

1 cinnamon stick

2 sprigs thyme

1½ cups/375 mL chopped canned
    tomatoes

1 cup/250 mL water

Salt and pepper

2 tbsp/25 mL raisins

1 preserved lemon, chopped

12 large green olives

Sea salt

4 6 oz/180 g halibut fillets, skinless

Chopped cilantro, for garnish

fish and tagine: Heat the oil in a large heavy saucepan over medium-high heat. Sauté the onions, carrots, potatoes, and squash for 6 to 10 minutes, stirring often.

- Add the ginger and garlic and sauté for a further 2 to 3 minutes. Stir in the coriander, turmeric, cumin, cinnamon, and thyme; cook for 6 to 8 minutes.
- Add the tomatoes and water and bring to a simmer. Season with salt and pepper and stir in the raisins. Cook for 20 to 25 minutes, until all the vegetables are soft to the touch. Just before serving, add the preserved lemon and the olives.
- Line the bottom of an Asian-style bamboo steamer with a piece of lightly oiled parchment paper. Place the halibut fillets on top, season them with a little sea salt, and steam them for 8 to 12 minutes, or until the fish is just cooked.
- To serve, place a good spoonful of the vegetables in a bowl with the steamed halibut on top. Garnish with freshly chopped cilantro and a sprinkle of dukkah.

cook's note: Although this recipe calls for steaming the halibut, it can also be pan fried, baked, or poached. Dukkah and preserved lemons can be purchased at Middle Eastern markets.

roasted Mediterranean sea bass on a seafood and green pea ragoût

Mediterranean sea bass, also known as spigola and branzino in Italy where it is hugely popular, was once the fish of the few because of its high price. Now, with carefully planned aquaculture, it is available to everyone and has become a staple in many North American restaurants. I like to serve it with a little fish and vegetable soup, commonly known as "in umido," from the Italian word for moist. *–Massimo*

serves 4

4 branzino, filleted
Salt and pepper
½ cup/125 mL olive oil, for drizzling
2 tbsp/25 mL olive oil
2 garlic cloves, chopped
1 red chili pepper, chopped
12 littleneck clams
½ cup/125 mL white wine
12 mussels
8 scampi, shelled
1 medium squid, cleaned and thinly sliced
1 cup/250 mL green peas
½ tsp/2 mL oregano leaves
1 cup/250 mL quartered red cherry tomatoes
2 tbsp/25 mL chopped parsley
2 tbsp/25 mL butter
Lemon, for garnish

- Preheat the oven to 375°F (190°C).

- Lightly grease a large baking dish with butter and oil. Season the branzino fillets with salt and pepper and drizzle a little olive oil—about 1 tbsp (15 mL)—on each one. Bake for 8 minutes, then remove the fish from the oven and cover it with foil to keep warm.
- Heat the 2 tbsp (25 mL) of olive oil in a saucepan over medium heat. Add the garlic, chili pepper, and the clams; sprinkle the wine over top. When the clams open, take them out of the pan with a slotted spoon and remove the meat from the shells. Set aside.
- In the same pan, cook the mussels until they open and remove the meat from the shells.
- Add the scampi, squid, peas, oregano, and tomatoes to the cooking liquid and simmer gently for 2 to 3 minutes. Add the parsley and butter, then return the clams and mussels to the pan. At this point, you should have a nice light seafood soup.
- Place the branzino on rimmed plates and scoop some seafood ragoût around the fillets. Squeeze a few drops of lemon juice on the fish, drizzle a little olive oil over the plate, and serve immediately.

herb crusted salmon with asparagus and citrus salad

At Peller, we're very conscientious about using seasonal, locally grown foods. But sometimes I get rebellious and use ingredients from further afield. This recipe, built around a citrus salad (not, obviously, grown in Niagara), was one of those times. Refreshing citrus is such a great accompaniment to the richness of salmon. *–Jason*

serves 4

¾ cup/175 mL roughly chopped parsley
½ cup/125 mL finely chopped shallots
¼ cup/50 mL roughly chopped tarragon
1 tbsp/15 mL cracked black pepper
1 tbsp/15 mL sea salt
¾ cup/175 mL olive oil
1 lb/500 g salmon fillet
¼ cup/50 mL lime juice
¼ cup/50 mL lemon juice
¼ cup/50 mL grapefruit juice
20 asparagus spears, blanched
1 cup/250 mL lime segments
1 cup/250 mL lemon segments
1 cup/250 mL grapefruit segments
4 cups/1 L arugula leaves
Salt and pepper

- In a bowl, combine the parsley, shallots, tarragon, cracked pepper, and sea salt with ¼ cup (50 mL) olive oil.
- Cut the salmon into four 4 oz (120 g) portions and spread the herb mixture on the flesh side of the fish.
- Heat another ¼ cup (50 mL) of the oil in a large skillet over medium-low heat. Place the salmon skin side down in the pan and cook slowly, until just cooked through (approximately 4 to 6 minutes).
- While the salmon is cooking, bring the lime, lemon, and grapefruit juices to a boil in a separate pan. Add the asparagus and the lime, lemon, and grapefruit segments, and return to a boil (if you cook it too long, the fruit will fall apart).
- Remove the salad from the heat and toss it with the arugula and the remaining oil. Season with salt and pepper and serve immediately.

maple roasted salmon
with bacon, corn, and blueberry potato cake

This was a recipe I wrote for the television show. Dramatic and flavourful, yet easy to make, it twists the Canadian content with the addition of the potato rösti. And it incorporates one of my favourite cooking techniques: the marriage of fish with cured meat. *—Jason*

serves 4

1 lb/500 g salmon fillet
2 tsp/10 mL grapeseed oil
2 tsp/10 mL maple syrup
2 tsp/10 mL butter
2 cups/500 mL diced potatoes, cooked
½ cup/125 mL diced bacon, cooked
½ cup/125 mL corn kernels
½ cup/125 mL dried blueberries
½ cup/125 mL grated Oka cheese
½ cup/125 mL crumbled goat cheese
Salt and pepper
2 cups/500 mL baby spinach
¼ cup/50 mL fresh blueberries

- Preheat the oven to 400°F (200°C).

- Cut the salmon into four 4 oz (120 g) portions.
- Heat 1 tsp (5 mL) of grapeseed oil in a skillet over medium-high heat. Sear the salmon for 1 minute, then turn it and add the maple syrup and butter.
- Transfer to the oven for 5 to 7 minutes, basting the salmon with the maple syrup and butter every minute or so.
- In a large bowl, combine the potatoes, bacon, corn, dried blueberries, and half the Oka and goat cheese. Season with salt and pepper and form into potato cakes. Chill in the refrigerator until firm.
- Heat the remaining grapeseed oil in a sauté pan and fry the potato cakes over medium-high heat until they're golden brown on both sides. Finish in the oven. When they're heated through, place one potato cake on each plate. Toss together the baby spinach, fresh blueberries, and the remaining Oka and goat cheese and place on the potato cakes. Top with the salmon and drizzle with any leftover maple butter.

cook's note: Dried blueberries are delicious but expensive. Dried cranberries make a tasty compromise.

6: bird feed

roasted chicken medallions
with prosciutto, Havarti, and peach jam

This is a dish that goes back to my time at the Millcroft Inn, when I was experimenting with chicken breasts and trying to find ways to change their shape and texture by pounding them out. Mild and creamy Havarti cheese is an obvious partner, but I love the way the peach jam caramelizes in the cooking, adding an additional level of flavour complexity. *–Jason*

serves 4

4 boneless, skinless chicken breasts
½ cup/125 mL peach jam
8 thin slices Havarti cheese
16 thin slices prosciutto
2 tbsp/25 mL grapeseed oil

- Preheat the oven to 350°F (180°C).

- Lay the chicken breasts between two pieces of plastic wrap and pound them out to about the thickness of a CD case.
- Cut each breast into four strips and place two end to end at a time to create one long strip. Spread the peach jam over the chicken, then add a layer of sliced Havarti. Roll up the strips like a pinwheel and secure them with bamboo skewers. Chill them in the refrigerator for 30 minutes until they're firm.
- Roll a slice of prosciutto around the outside of each chicken medallion and chill.
- Heat the grapeseed oil in a skillet over medium-high heat. Sear both sides of the medallions until golden brown, then finish in the oven for 5 to 7 minutes, until the chicken is cooked through. Let stand for 3 minutes before serving.

grilled chicken paillard on summer greens

This flexible, quick, and easy recipe is open to endless variation: summer greens come in all shapes and sizes, from the inner leaves of celery stalks to dandelion, spinach, and peppery watercress. Slices of ripe pear, peach, or apple are welcome additions. Or you could mix the crunch of cucumber with the creaminess of avocado for an array of colour, taste, and texture that is perfect for al fresco dining. *–Michael*

serves 2

for the salsa verde:
¼ cup/50 mL raw almonds
3 cloves garlic, chopped
1 cup/250 mL parsley
½ cup/125 mL basil leaves
½ cup/125 mL cilantro leaves
¼ cup/50 mL mint leaves
¼ cup/50 mL capers
4 anchovy fillets (optional)
¼ tsp/1 mL chili flakes
1 cup/250 mL olive oil
¼ cup/50 mL sherry vinegar
Salt and pepper

salsa verde: Preheat the oven to 375°F (190°C).

- Scatter the almonds on a pie plate and dry roast them for 8 to 10 minutes, stirring occasionally, until golden brown. Cool.
- Pulse three or four times in a food processor along with the garlic, until roughly chopped. Add the parsley, basil, cilantro, mint, capers, anchovies, chili flakes, and a splash of the olive oil and pulse three or four more times. Add the sherry vinegar and season with salt and pepper. While pulsing, slowly and continuously drizzle in the remaining olive oil, until the salsa is the texture of pesto.
- Remove from the food processor, adjust for seasoning, and store in an airtight container for at least 2 hours to allow the flavours to blend. Serve at room temperature.

for the dressing:

⅓ cup/90 mL good olive oil

3 tbsp/45 mL lemon juice

Splash white wine vinegar

¼ tsp/1 mL dry mustard

Salt and pepper

for the paillard:

2 6 oz/175 g boneless, skinless
    chicken breasts

Salt and pepper

2 tbsp/25 mL olive oil

Pinch thyme leaves

2 handfuls mixed greens
    (watercress, arugula, dandelion,
    mizuna, rainbow chard)

1 cup/250 mL mixed herbs
    (mint, basil, chervil, chives)

½ cucumber, peeled, seeded,
    and thinly sliced

12 cherry tomatoes

1 tbsp/15 mL crumbled goat cheese

1 lemon, halved

dressing: Whisk together the olive oil, lemon juice, vinegar, mustard, and salt and pepper to taste; let rest to meld the flavours.

paillard: Place the chicken breasts between two pieces of plastic wrap and pound them flat (or ask your butcher to do it for you). Season lightly with salt and pepper then rub them with the olive oil and a sprinkle of thyme. Set aside.

- In a large bowl, combine the salad greens with the mixed herbs, cucumber, cherry tomatoes, and goat cheese; toss lightly. Drizzle the dressing over the salad, toss well, and divide between two serving plates.
- Cook the chicken paillards over high heat on the barbecue or in a grill pan. The paillards will cook very quickly, needing just 1 to 2 minutes on each side.
- Place one paillard on top of each salad, garnish with half a lemon, and serve with a generous spoonful of salsa verde.

cook's note: The salsa verde can be paired with any grilled meat or seafood.

country style pot-roast chicken with sherry

Ten years ago while travelling in southern Spain, I visited a sherry producer, where we were served a dish very similar to this. The distinctive rustic flavours of the sherry and sherry vinegar still linger in my memory. Pomegranates hanging from trees, olive groves in the distance, and chickens roaming freely among the vines were my inspiration. I remember the appetizer was fresh orange: picked that morning, drizzled with olive oil, and sprinkled with thinly shredded fennel. –*Michael*

serves 4

1 3½ lb/1.75 kg chicken, cut into pieces
Salt and pepper
2 tbsp/25 mL olive oil
10 pearl onions, peeled
1 cup/250 mL mushrooms
2 cups/500 mL diced canned tomatoes
1 sprig thyme
¼ cup/50 mL sherry
¼ cup/50 mL sherry vinegar
⅓ cup/75 mL chicken stock
1 14 oz/398 g can artichoke hearts, drained and quartered
½ cup/125 mL black olives

- Preheat the oven to 350°F (180°C).

- Season the chicken pieces with salt and pepper.
- Heat the olive oil in a large sauté pan over medium-high heat. Sauté the chicken, turning often, until golden brown. Add the pearl onions and mushrooms and cook for 2 to 3 minutes. Add the tomatoes, thyme, half the sherry, half the sherry vinegar, and the chicken stock. The liquid should come only halfway up the chicken.
- Season with salt and pepper and place in the oven with the chicken skin side up. Roast for 20 to 30 minutes without turning the chicken—this will allow the skin to become crispy. For the last 5 minutes, turn on the broiler, move the chicken close to the broiler, and allow it to crispen and blister.
- Remove from the oven and skim off any excess oil. Stir in the artichoke quarters, olives, and the remaining 2 tbsp (25 mL) sherry and sherry vinegar and serve.

Niagara coq au vin

In many ways, working in Niagara reminds me of my classical French training in which wine played such a key role. Here at Peller, of course, wine informs everything that we do. So what makes more sense than a classic French recipe made with local ingredients and our own wine? The cocoa powder is the secret ingredient here, giving the sauce a depth and complexity that just isn't possible from the wine and stock alone. *–Jason*

serves 4

2 shallots, roughly chopped

1 medium carrot, roughly chopped

½ bunch thyme

2 cloves garlic, roughly chopped

1 bottle (750 mL) full-bodied red wine

1 tbsp/15 mL cocoa powder

4 1½ lb/750 g chickens, cut into
    pieces

2 tbsp/25 mL grapeseed oil

4 cups/1 L beef stock

12 baby carrots

12 pearl onions

12 button mushrooms

2 tbsp/25 mL bacon

12 asparagus spears

- Combine the shallots, chopped carrot, thyme, garlic, wine, and cocoa powder. Pour over the chicken, cover, and marinate in the refrigerator for 24 hours.
- Drain the chicken and vegetables, preserving the marinade.
- Heat the oil in a large pot over medium-high heat and brown the chicken, about 3 minutes each side. Remove the chicken and set aside.
- Add the reserved marinade, reducing by half. Pour in the beef stock and bring to a simmer. Strain the liquid and return it to the pot along with the baby carrots, pearl onions, button mushrooms, bacon, and chicken. Simmer for approximately 25 minutes, until the chicken is cooked through, adding the asparagus in the last 5 minutes.
- Let the chicken rest for 3 to 5 minutes before serving.

cook's note: I buy *poussin* chickens, which are young birds with a maximum weight of 1½ lbs (750 g).

pot-roasted Cornish hens with mushrooms and tarragon cream

This is a classic French bistro dish that is often served with green beans, mashed potatoes, and a simple salad. It can be served family style or individually plated. Cornish hen (like most meats) is moist and delicious when roasted whole on the bone. *—Michael*

serves 4

2 Cornish hens, approximately
    1 lb/500 g each
Salt and pepper
1 tbsp/15 mL vegetable oil
24 pearl onions or small shallots,
    peeled
2 cloves garlic, crushed
1 sprig thyme
2 cups/500 mL button mushrooms
1 cup/250 mL dry white wine
1½ cups/375 mL whipping (35%)
    cream
1 tbsp/15 mL lemon juice
1 tsp/5 mL chopped fresh tarragon

- Preheat the oven to 350°F (180°C).

- Season the hens liberally with salt and pepper, inside and out.
- In a heavy Dutch oven, heat the oil over high heat. Brown the hens on each side, turning every 2 or 3 minutes. Add the pearl onions, garlic, and thyme.
- Roast in the oven for 6 to 8 minutes. Turn the heat down to 325°F (160°C) and cook for an additional 6 to 8 minutes. Add the mushrooms and continue cooking for another 5 minutes.
- Remove the pot from the oven and return it to the stovetop. Pour in the white wine and simmer for 2 or 3 minutes. Stir in the cream, lemon juice, and tarragon; season the sauce with salt and pepper. As the sauce is simmering and reducing slightly, spoon some over the chicken occasionally.
- Once the sauce is thick enough to coat the back of a spoon, turn off the heat, cover, and let rest for 10 minutes before serving.

Cornish hens stuffed with lobster and asparagus

I love cooking these little birds: the size is perfect for a shared dinner, and they seem so much more special than plain old chicken. The creaminess of the béchamel creates the perfect bridge between the meat and the seafood, and the flavour the prosciutto gives to the bird as it cooks is fantastic. *–Massimo*

serves 4

for the béchamel:
¼ cup/50 mL butter
⅓ cup/75 mL all-purpose flour
1½ cups/375 mL milk
1 cup/250 mL grated Grana Padano cheese (or Parmigiano-Reggiano)

for the hens:
3 tbsp/45 mL olive oil
¼ cup/50 mL minced vegetables (a mix of celery, onion, carrot, garlic, and parsley)
½ cup/125 mL béchamel sauce
¼ cup/50 mL grated Grana Padano cheese
2 egg yolks
12 oz/375 g chopped lobster meat
10 asparagus spears, blanched and cut on the diagonal into 2-inch/5 cm lengths
2 Cornish hens, cut in half
Salt and pepper
8 very thin slices prosciutto
1 tbsp/15 mL butter
½ cup/125 mL white wine
½ cup/125 mL chicken stock

- Preheat the oven to 450°F (230°C).

béchamel: Melt the butter with the flour in a saucepan over medium heat, mixing well, until it takes on a light golden colour. Remove from the heat and cool for a minute.
- In a separate pan, bring the milk to a boil, then add it to the butter and flour, stirring well to prevent lumps. Return to a boil, lower heat, and simmer for 20 minutes. Remove from the heat and add the cheese. Mix well and set aside.

hens: Heat 1 tbsp (15 mL) of the oil in a small skillet over medium heat and sauté the minced vegetables until soft, about 3 minutes. Set aside.
- Combine the béchamel, cheese, and egg yolks with the vegetables. Mix well to form a paste, then stir in the lobster meat and asparagus.
- Carefully remove the breast and thigh bones from the hens. Fill each half with stuffing, season the birds with salt and pepper, then fold the breast and roll it like a cigar. Wrap the hens with prosciutto and chill in the refrigerator for at least 2 hours.
- Heat the remaining oil and the butter in a skillet on medium-high heat. Sear the birds on all sides, then sprinkle with the wine and let it evaporate. Pour in the stock and roast in the oven for approximately 15 minutes until the juices run clear when the birds are pierced between the thigh and body.

pheasant in umido with chiodini mushrooms

The best way to enjoy pheasant is to hunt it yourself, but it's not really necessary these days, when they're widely available in quality butcher stores. "In umido" simply means cooked with moisture, rather than dry roasted. Meat cooked in this way is generally served with soft polenta or mashed potatoes. *—Massimo*

serves 4

2 tbsp/25 mL olive oil

1 tbsp/15 mL butter

4 pheasant breasts, about 8 oz/250 g
    each, skin on

Salt and pepper

1 bouquet garni with rosemary, sage,
    thyme

1 cup/250 mL finely cut pancetta

½ cup/125 mL chopped onions

2 cloves garlic, minced

2 cups/500 mL chiodini mushrooms

½ cup/125 mL white wine

2 cups/500 mL peeled, seeded,
    and chopped fresh tomatoes

1 cup/250 mL chicken stock,
    if needed

- Heat the olive oil and butter in a skillet on medium-high heat.
- Season the pheasant with salt and pepper and place in the skillet, breast side down. Toss in the bouquet garni and sear the pheasant on both sides until golden. Add the pancetta, onions, and garlic; cook until translucent. Stir in the mushrooms and cook until soft, then sprinkle in the wine and let it evaporate completely. Add the tomatoes and simmer for 5 minutes, adding chicken stock if necessary for moisture. Remove the breasts and cover with foil to keep warm.
- Cook the sauce for 3 to 5 minutes longer, until it's nice and creamy. Return the pheasant to the skillet and simmer gently until the breasts are thoroughly cooked.

cook's note: Chiodini mushrooms are also known as shimeji, but any wild foraged or flavourful mushrooms work well, and in a pinch cremini are just fine.

individual turkey pot pie

I love turkey, but I'm not a big fan of leftovers. So for me this is the perfect way of gathering up all the leftovers from a holiday dinner and turning them into something special for another meal. –*Jason*

serves 5

for the pastry:
3 cups/750 mL cake and pastry flour
1¼ cups/300 mL shortening
2 tbsp/25 mL brown sugar
1 tbsp/15 mL salt
⅔ cup/150 mL cold water

for the pies:
Pie dough to line and cover 5
    4-inch/10 cm springform pans
¼ cup/50 mL butter
½ cup/125 mL sliced shallots
3 garlic cloves, chopped
3 cups/750 mL sliced mushrooms
    (any mix of shiitake, portobello,
    oyster)
Salt and pepper
½ cup/125 mL chopped bacon
1 cup/250 mL chopped Brussels
    sprouts
1 cup/250 mL diced cooked potatoes
¼ cup/50 mL roughly chopped sage
    leaves
2 cups/500 mL turkey gravy
2 cups/500 mL shredded roasted
    turkey meat

- Preheat the oven to 350°F (180°C).

pastry: Crumble the flour and shortening in a large bowl.
- In a separate bowl, dissolve the sugar and salt into the water. Slowly mix the water solution into the flour and shortening to form a soft dough.
- Cover with plastic wrap and chill in the refrigerator for at least 45 minutes.

pies: Line the springform pans with two thirds of the pastry.
- Melt 2 tbsp (25 mL) of butter in a skillet over medium-high heat. Sauté the shallots and garlic without allowing to colour for 1 minute. Add the mushrooms and sauté until cooked through. Season with salt and pepper and distribute among the pie pans.
- In a separate skillet, melt the remaining 2 tbsp (25 mL) of butter over medium-high heat. Add the bacon and sauté for 2 minutes, then add the Brussels sprouts, potatoes, and sage, continuing to sauté until warmed through. Season the potatoes and sprouts with salt and pepper and layer evenly over the mushrooms.
- In a third pot, warm the turkey gravy and mix with the cooked turkey meat. Scatter the meat over the potatoes and sprouts to fill the pie. Cover with the remaining pastry and pinch the two pieces of dough together. Chill in the refrigerator for 30 minutes.
- Bake the pies in the oven for 12 to 15 minutes. Let rest for 2 to 3 minutes before serving.

pan-roasted quails with pancetta

I'm not kidding when I say I was brought up on a 100-foot diet. Our family kept hundreds of chickens, geese, guinea fowls, rabbits, and quails. One of my favourite childhood meals was quail wrapped in pancetta and stuffed with a few garlic cloves and lots of rosemary, served with potatoes from the sandy soil by the river. –*Massimo*

serves 4

8 jumbo quails
3 sprigs rosemary
3 sprigs sage
3 sprigs thyme
Salt and pepper
16 slices pancetta
2 tbsp/25 mL olive oil
2 tbsp/25 mL butter
½ cup/125 mL minced celery
½ cup/125 mL minced carrots
½ cup/125 mL minced onions
4 bay leaves
8 garlic cloves, crushed
1 cup/250 mL white wine

- Preheat the oven to 475°F (240°C).

- Wash and dry the quails and set aside.
- Shred the fresh herbs and stuff them in the chest cavities of the birds with some salt and pepper. Wrap each bird with at least two strips of pancetta (use more if needed).
- Heat the oil and butter in a sauté pan large enough to fit the birds snugly. Cook the minced celery, carrots, and onions along with the bay leaves and garlic until the garlic is translucent.
- Place the quails in the pan on their backs with the legs towards the centre of the pan. Sear them for 1 minute, then cover the pan with a tight-fitting lid and roast in the oven for about 6 minutes. Remove the lid and sprinkle the wine over the birds. Cook, uncovered, for 10 minutes longer.
- Remove from the oven, cover, and let rest for 10 minutes before serving.

duck pot roast with mostarda di Cremona

Mostarda is a condiment made of candied fruit in mustard-flavoured syrup. Mostarda di Cremona is the most famous version. Look for a pungent style, with lots of mustard heat–without it, it's just not as good and comes across like some kind of weird jam. Mostarda is traditionally eaten with boiled or roasted meats, cheese, and bread. –*Massimo*

serves 4

1 young duck, about 5 lbs/2.5 kg
Salt and pepper
2 tbsp/25 mL olive oil
1 cup/250 mL diced celery
1 cup/250 mL diced carrots
1 cup/250 mL diced onions
4 cloves garlic, chopped
1 cup/250 mL white wine
2 tbsp/25 mL tomato paste
2 cups/500 mL chicken stock
2 bay leaves
2 cups sliced mostarda di Cremona

- Season the duck with salt and pepper and, using a meat fork (or needles), pierce as many holes in the skin as possible.
- Heat the oil in a heavy pot over high heat and sauté the celery, carrots, onions, and garlic until the vegetables are soft. Remove from the pot with a slotted spoon and set aside. Sear the duck in the same pot for 5 minutes on each side, then remove the excess fat and return the vegetables. Pour in the wine and let it evaporate, then add the tomato paste and mix well.
- Season with salt and pepper and add the stock and bay leaves. Roast in the oven for 1 hour, or until the legs are tender. Remove the duck and wrap it in foil to keep warm.
- Skim off as much fat from the sauce as you can, remove the bay leaves, and use a stick blender to emulsify the sauce. Strain it through a fine mesh strainer and set aside.
- Serve some of the leg and some of the breast to each person or serve it family style on a platter so everyone can choose their own. Put a little of the mostarda on top, with more on the side for seconds.

early days: *Jason Parsons*

I didn't always love food. When I was a young boy, my family lived in the English countryside, surrounded by some of the best ingredients you could imagine. Farms as far as the eye could see and I had no appetite for any of it. I remember sitting in the doctor's office hearing, "Jason, if you don't put fuel in the car, the car won't work." But all I would eat was eggs or broiled chicken breast. Little did I know that food would become my life.

I remember the day my parents sat my brother and me down to announce we were moving to Canada. I was nine, my brother 13. I think my first question was, "Do they have TV there?" My brother was next, with questions about bears and log cabins. We were clueless.

I think my strength to this day comes from having watched my parents give up everything they had in England—my dad as an executive at a big car company and my mom as a social worker for families in need—giving up the security of everything for the dream of importing antiques into Canada and owning their own store.

My first job, not counting the odd paper route, was working at Lulu's Roadhouse. One night my brother, who worked

there, called: "We desperately need busboys to wash glasses. It's only for a few weeks." I was not yet 14 and my mom wasn't keen on the idea of me working in a bar, but she did not want to squash my excitement. My cousin and I started at the same time, and soon more of my friends followed. We all learned quickly what work was all about. Of course, once in the door, a few weeks became a few more, and after six months I found myself working in the kitchen as a prep cook.

This was my first taste of a kitchen. Looking back now I know I was a long way from the gourmet kitchens of the world, but I took all the drive I'd learned from working in my parents' shop and put it toward making that kitchen my own. Within six months I was kitchen manager, supplying the chefs on the grill with enough food to serve hundreds. I can remember cleaning case after case of lettuce, baking tray after tray of potatoes, and roasting up to 30 prime ribs a night. This was a great time for me: working with friends, running what felt like my own little business.

But it wasn't long before I wanted to be like the chefs up on the grill. Lulu's had an open grill, and this was where the cool guys were. Working the grill, balancing all the orders, plating the food—always aware of the customers directly in front of them. The head chef, Richard, was cocky, full of life, and could work the huge grill better than anyone else. I remember him showing me how to organize my own grill. The steaks would all enter from the left, and I would move them across the coals as they went from rare to medium rare, medium, and so on. I was able to serve a small army and cook every steak to perfection while still glazing the ribs, carving the prime rib, and microwaving the lobster tails. Yes, that's right, microwaving. I did say it was a roadhouse. I learned how to organize myself, but I was a long way from real cooking. I didn't care, though. I was truly in my element, in control. The four years I spent at Lulu's softened the blow later, when I entered the hard-core world of fine dining.

I remember looking up the driveway at the yet-to-be-finished Langdon Hall and thinking, "If I can just get a job in the kitchen I will soon work my way up to kitchen manager again." I was on my way to my first meeting with Geoffrey Bray-Cotton, who became a lifelong friend. So far the interviews had gone well, but the next was with a small intense man, chef Nigel Didcock, who would change my life. I really don't remember exactly how it went, but I do remember talking about an apprenticeship and Chef trying to talk me out of it. But the more he said, the more I wanted it. I left there with a full apprenticeship, a mentor, and a future. I was terrified but had never felt more excited.

I soon found out I wasn't terrified enough. Chef Didcock was the protege of Michel Bourdin, one of the godfathers of gastronomy. Didcock taught me that high standards are the most important thing. Not only does the finished plate have to be perfect, but so does everything that leads up to it—where the ingredients are from, how they are stored, prepared, and cooked. Food is to be respected at every stage of its journey, from its glorious beginning to its glorious end. The basics are the core of every great chef. This is where I developed my passion for food.

The next three and half years were some of the most challenging times of my life, but I truly felt part of something special. I graduated from high school and culinary school, completed a full apprenticeship, and received my chef's papers. These were my tickets to the world.

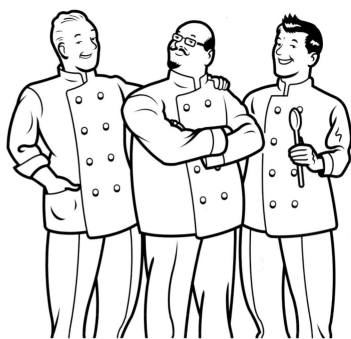

7: meat market

Muskoka barbecue sauce

This all-purpose summer barbecue sauce, a classic for ribs, chicken, or flank steak, is a favourite at our house. You can double up the recipe and freeze the extra in plastic containers so you always have some on hand. It will keep well in the refrigerator for two or three weeks if properly sealed. *–Michael*

makes about 2 cups (500 mL)

¼ cup/50 mL vegetable oil
1½ large onions, diced
6 cloves garlic, sliced
1½ cups/375 mL drained and
    chopped canned tomatoes
¾ cup/175 mL balsamic vinegar
½ cup/125 mL tomato paste
½ cup/125 mL brown sugar
¼ cup/50 mL Worcestershire sauce
3 tbsp/45 mL dry mustard
2½ tbsp/30 mL chipotle peppers in
    adobo sauce
2 tsp/10 mL kosher salt
1 tbsp/15 mL dried thyme
1 tbsp/15 mL dried sage
1 tbsp/15 mL dried basil
1½ tsp/7 mL smoked paprika

- Heat the vegetable oil in a sauté pan over medium-high heat. Fry the onions and garlic until light golden brown, about 12 to 15 minutes. Add the tomatoes and balsamic vinegar; cook for another 10 to 12 minutes. Stir in the tomato paste, brown sugar, Worcestershire sauce, chipotle peppers, and mustard. Continue cooking for another 5 to 7 minutes, then add the salt, thyme, sage, basil, and paprika. Simmer gently for 20 minutes, adding splashes of water as needed if the sauce becomes too thick.
- Remove from the heat and cool. Purée in a blender, then strain through a sieve into a clean pot.
- Return to the heat and simmer for 1 to 2 minutes, again adjusting the thickness with water if necessary.
- Cool, pour into jars, cover, and refrigerate.

Cadillac grill barbecue rub

We bought our first real barbecue for our Blue Mountain restaurant in Collingwood. It was custom made in Arkansas by a guy named Robert Post. We flew Robert in for the christening, and he cooked the best beef brisket I've ever tasted. Controlling the damper, working the moisture levels, stoking the embers were all part of the fun. When everything was in perfect harmony, Robert would say, "She's Cadillac-ing." The phrase stuck and we named our favourite dry rub for it. –*Michael*

makes about 2 cups (500 mL)

¼ cup/50 mL chili powder
¼ cup/50 mL paprika
¼ cup/50 mL smoked paprika
3 tbsp/45 mL salt
2½ tbsp/30 mL garam masala
   (mild curry power)
2 tbsp/25 mL dry mustard
2 tbsp/25 mL granulated sugar
2 tbsp/25 mL ground coriander
1 tbsp/15 mL cayenne pepper
1 tbsp/15 mL ground cumin
1 tbsp/15 mL dried thyme
1 tbsp/15 mL dried basil
1 tbsp/15 mL pepper

- Combine all the ingredients in a 500 mL Mason jar. Close the lid securely and shake well to blend.

pan-fried Berkshire pork chops with red cabbage and apple chutney

Berkshire pork, known for its well-marbled fat and the flavour and tenderness that results, is increasingly popular. It always does very well on our menus. Although this dish has a slightly autumnal feel, it can be made any time red cabbage is available. –*Michael*

serves 4

for the apple chutney:
4 tart apples, peeled, cored, and
    chopped
1 onion, quartered
1 thumb-sized piece ginger, peeled
¼ cup/50 mL white wine
2 tbsp/25 mL granulated sugar
2 tbsp/25 mL brown sugar
Pinch each cinnamon, white pepper,
    ground cardamom, and nutmeg

for the red cabbage:
¼ cup/50 mL vegetable oil
½ medium red cabbage, thinly sliced
2 medium carrots, grated
1 crisp green apple, grated
Salt and pepper
1½ tsp/7 mL caraway seeds
½ cup/125 mL apple cider vinegar
½ cup/125 mL apple juice
¾ cup/175 mL cranberries

for the pork chops:
4 Berkshire pork chops
Salt and pepper
1 tbsp/15 mL butter
Olive oil

apple chutney: Combine all the ingredients in a saucepan and bring to a boil. Reduce heat and cover. Simmer for 20 minutes, stirring frequently, until the apples are tender, adding water if necessary to keep the ingredients moist. Remove the onion and ginger and chill in the refrigerator until ready to serve.

red cabbage: In a large stainless steel pot, bring the oil, cabbage, carrots, and apple to a simmer over medium-high heat. Season with salt and pepper, then add the caraway, vinegar, and apple juice. Partially cover and cook for 18 to 25 minutes. During the last 10 minutes, add the cranberries and stir occasionally. Remove from the heat and cool before serving.

pork chops: Season the chops with salt and pepper. Heat the butter and a splash of olive oil over medium heat, then gently sauté the pork. Turn occasionally until they are cooked to just pink and tender.

assembly: Place a mound of the red cabbage just off-centre on each plate. Lean the pork chop on the red cabbage and garnish it with a spoonful of the apple chutney.

baby back ribs with maple-tomato baked beans

To me, there's something so Canadian about this dish, with its back bacon and maple-baked beans. Along with some corn on the cob and homemade coleslaw, it's the perfect end to an active summer day—I love it after a day on the water at the cottage. *–Michael*

serves 4

for the beans:
1 tsp/5 mL canola oil

8 oz/250 g Canadian back bacon, cut into lardons

1 large onion, chopped

1 lb/500 g navy beans, soaked overnight

6 cups/1.5 L hot water

½ cup/125 mL ketchup

¼ cup/50 mL molasses

¼ cup/50 mL maple syrup

1 tbsp/15 mL tomato paste

3 cloves garlic, minced

1 tbsp/15 mL dry mustard

Salt and pepper

- Preheat the oven to 300°F (150°C).

beans: Heat the canola oil in a saucepan over medium heat. Sauté the bacon until it's golden brown, about 10 to 15 minutes. Add the onions and sauté for 3 to 4 minutes. Drain the beans and place them in a covered earthenware or casserole dish along with the bacon and onion mixture.

- In a bowl, combine the water, ketchup, molasses, maple syrup, tomato paste, garlic, mustard, and salt and pepper to taste. Add to the beans and mix well. Cover and bake in the oven for 3 hours.

- Uncover and continue to cook for 1 hour, or until the beans are tender and the sauce has thickened.

for the ribs:

2 full racks baby back ribs

¾ tsp/3 mL smoked paprika

Salt and pepper

2½ cups/625 mL barbecue sauce

1½ cups/375 mL beef broth

1 medium onion, roughly chopped

3 cloves garlic, crushed

1 bay leaf

- Preheat the barbecue on medium high.

ribs: Cut the racks in half and rub both sides with the paprika. Season them lightly with salt and pepper.

- In a heavy, shallow roasting pan, combine the barbecue sauce, beef broth, onion, garlic, and bay leaf. Mix thoroughly.

- Place the ribs on a rack inside the roasting pan so they sit just above the liquid. Cover the pan with foil and cook the ribs on the barbecue for 2 to 2½ hours, basting every 15 minutes with the pan liquids. Turn the ribs two or three times. When they're cooked, your liquid will be reduced to a nice glaze. To test if the ribs are done, simply pull on a bone: it should come away with little effort.

- When the ribs are cooked, remove the pan from the barbecue and let them rest for 15 to 20 minutes. Transfer the ribs back to the barbecue and grill them for 3 to 4 minutes on each side while basting with the reduced glaze from the pan.

- Pour any remaining sauce into a bowl and serve it alongside the ribs.

chardonnay-braised lamb shank

I don't think enough people realize how good—and easy to prepare—slow-braised meat on the bone is. In Europe, most home cooks are very comfortable with the "off cuts," but in North America we still have a ways to go. Maybe this dish, with its perfect balance of comfort and freshness, will help. I'm a big believer in using white wine when cooking lamb: it doesn't overwhelm the delicate flavour of the meat the way red wine can. *–Jason*

serves 4

1 tbsp/15 mL grapeseed oil
4 lamb shanks
½ cup/125 mL chopped carrots
½ cup/125 mL chopped leeks
½ cup/125 mL chopped celery
¼ cup/50 mL chopped onions
1 clove garlic, crushed
¼ cup/50 mL chopped tomato
½ tsp/2 mL fennel seed
½ tsp/2 mL white peppercorns
3 sprigs thyme
1 cup/250 mL chardonnay wine
    (or other full-bodied white)
3 cups/750 mL beef stock
Salt and pepper

- Preheat the oven to 425°F (220°C).

- Heat the oil in a large, heavy pot over medium-high heat. Sear the lamb shanks on all sides until golden brown. Remove from the pot and set aside.
- Add the carrots, leeks, celery, onions, and garlic, and sauté until browned. Add the tomatoes, fennel, peppercorns, thyme, and wine. Simmer until reduced to one quarter, then add the stock and the lamb.
- Bring to a simmer, cover, and roast in the oven for 45 to 60 minutes. When the meat pulls away from the bone, remove the pot from the oven and let rest for 5 minutes before serving.
- For the sauce, strain the braising juices and simmer until they are reduced by half. Season to taste with salt and pepper.

lamb chop Milanese with tomato confit

What could be more satisfying than this for lunch? I went to cooking school in a town called Salsomaggiore that was about an hour and a half from my home town near Cremona. On the days we didn't have lunch at school, I would get home at around 3 PM, hungry as a wolf, and this, along with an arugula salad topped with shaved Parmesan cheese, was my lunch of choice. –*Massimo*

serves 4 to 5

for the tomato confit:
1 lb/500 g plum tomatoes
2 cups/500 mL chopped onions
2 cloves garlic, crushed
6 basil leaves
1 tsp/5 mL granulated sugar
2 tbsp/25 mL red wine vinegar
⅓ cup/75 mL olive oil

for the lamb:
2 lamb racks, cut into chops
⅔ cup/150 mL Parmigiano-Reggiano cheese
1½ cups/375 g fresh bread crumbs
Salt and pepper
2 eggs, beaten
⅓ cup/75 mL milk
1 cup/250 mL all-purpose flour
Olive oil, as needed
Butter, as needed

confit: Combine all the ingredients in a saucepan and cook until dense and ketchup-like. Season to taste, then refrigerate for 24 hours to allow the flavours to blend.

lamb: Cut the lamb into chops. If necessary, use a mallet to even out the thickness—ideally ¼ inch (5 mm).
- Mix the Parmigiano and the bread crumbs on a plate and season with salt and pepper.
- Combine the eggs and milk; beat lightly.
- Dredge the lamb in the flour, coating it evenly. Dip it in the egg wash and then the breading. Press the crumbs into the lamb to ensure an even coating.
- Fry the chops in a skillet on medium-high heat. You'll need to do this in batches: start with 1 tbsp (15 mL) each of butter and olive oil and replenish as necessary.

veal brisket with roasted baby vegetables

This is a recipe that has family meal written all over it. I have many good memories of waking up late on Sunday mornings and walking into the kitchen, guided by the smell of gently roasting garlic and rosemary. Mom always made me a prince's breakfast, and I had nothing but free time on my hands until the big family meal in the afternoon. *–Massimo*

serves 6 to 8

for the brisket:

1 veal brisket, trimmed of fat and ready to roast (ask your butcher to prepare it)

Salt and pepper

2 cups/500 mL diced onions

1 cup/250 mL diced celery

1 cup/250 mL diced carrots

4 cloves garlic

2 bunches each of rosemary, sage, and thyme

2 tbsp/25 mL olive oil

2 tbsp/25 mL butter, softened

2 cups/500 mL chicken stock

2 cups/500 mL white wine

Water, as needed

¼ cup/50 mL whipping (35%) cream

2 tbsp/25 mL Pommery mustard

1 tbsp/15 mL honey

Juice of ½ lemon

for the vegetables:

8 green asparagus tips

8 white asparagus tips

8 baby cauliflower

4 baby green zucchini

4 baby yellow zucchini

8 baby carrots, halved lengthwise

4 baby golden beets, cooked

Olive oil

Salt and pepper

- Preheat the oven to 450°F (230°C).

brisket: Season the brisket with salt and pepper and sear in a preheated skillet until golden brown. Place the onions, celery, carrots, garlic, and fresh herbs in a baking pan with the meat on top. Drizzle the oil over top and spread the butter on the meat. Roast for approximately 30 minutes.

- Reduce the heat to 325°F (160°C) and continue cooking for about 1½ hours, turning the meat occasionally and moistening with the stock and wine a little at a time. By the end of this stage, the roast should be almost cooked.
- Scoop the juices from the bottom of the pan and pour them over the meat every 10 minutes for another half hour, or until the meat is tender to the fork. It is tedious work but worthwhile—the result is a tender, glossy roast full of flavour.
- Remove from the oven, wrap the meat in foil, and strain the juices, adding a bit of water, if necessary, to make them run. Simmer the jus on medium heat. Add the cream, mustard, and honey; reduce the liquid by a third. Squeeze in the lemon juice and set aside.

- Increase the heat to 500°F (260°C).

vegetables: Place all the vegetables in a bowl and dress with oil, salt, and pepper. Spread them on a baking sheet and roast in the oven for about 15 minutes, or until soft, stirring every 5 minutes.

veal T-bone with mushroom ragoût, melted leeks, and blue cheese

This dish—basically an upscale take on steak and mushrooms—is deliberately masculine. It's the veal equivalent of a Porterhouse steak, and it's extremely popular with many of the men who come to our restaurants. With the T-bone you get some of the loin and tenderloin, but you have to work at navigating the bone, which keeps it all together and adds tons of flavour. *–Michael*

serves 4

4 1 lb/500 g veal T-bone steaks
Salt and pepper
2 tbsp/25 mL olive oil
1 clove garlic, crushed
1 shallot, diced
8 cups/2 L coarsely diced mixed
    mushrooms
2 tsp/10 mL butter
3 cups/750 mL leeks, sliced into rings
½ cup/125 mL whipping (35%) cream
¼ cup/50 mL Stilton cheese
Chives, for garnish
1 lemon, cut in 4 wedges

- Preheat the oven to 375°F (190°C).

- Season the veal with salt and pepper. Heat the olive oil in a heavy pan over medium-high heat and sauté the T-bones, browning them on all sides. Finish in the oven for 3 to 5 minutes until medium-rare or medium. Remove from the pan, cover with foil, and let rest.
- In the same pan, toss in the garlic, shallots, and mushrooms. Season well with salt and pepper and sauté quickly.
- In a separate pan, melt the butter, then add the leeks, cream, and salt and pepper. Simmer gently for 4 to 5 minutes or until the leeks are tender. Add the Stilton, stir once or twice, and it is ready to serve.
- Divide the mushrooms among the plates and top with the T-bones. Spoon the melted leeks and cheese over top. Sprinkle with chives and garnish with a wedge of lemon.

Ontario veal rib-eye with peach and corn ragoût

This is our number one seller each fall, and it's all about the ripe peaches and corn, which go together so wonderfully in the ragoût. Their complementary/contrasting sweetness, balanced by the smokiness of the veal bacon, sets off the subtle flavour of the rib-eye perfectly. —Jason

serves 6

for the rib-eye:

1 lb/500 g veal rib-eye
12 very thin slices veal bacon
1 tbsp/15 mL grapeseed oil

for the peach ragoût:

1 tbsp/15 mL butter
¼ cup/50 mL diced veal bacon
¼ cup/50 mL sliced shallots
½ cup/125 mL corn kernels
2 tbsp/25 mL chopped rosemary
¼ cup/50 mL riesling icewine (or other late-harvest white)
½ cup/125 mL diced peaches
½ cup/125 mL whipping (35%) cream
½ cup/125 mL triple-cream Brie cheese
Salt and pepper

- Preheat the oven to 400°F (200°C).

rib-eye: Lay a large square of plastic wrap flat on the counter and place the bacon down its centre. Place the veal on top of the bacon. Using the plastic, roll the bacon around the veal to form a cylinder. Wrap tightly and chill for 15 minutes.

- Cut into four portions and remove the plastic.
- Heat the oil in a large oven-proof skillet over high heat. Sear the veal until golden brown on all sides.
- Transfer the pan to the oven and roast for 12 to 15 minutes, then remove it and let the meat rest for 3 minutes before serving it over the ragoût.

ragoût: Melt the butter in a skillet over medium-high heat. Add the bacon and shallots, then sauté for about 1 minute, just long enough to release the flavours.

- Add the corn, rosemary, and icewine; warm through. Stir in the peaches and cream. When hot, add the Brie and remove from the heat. Allow the cheese to soften, then season with salt and pepper.

red wine–braised beef short ribs

These hugely satisfying ribs are great with mashed potatoes, buttered new potatoes, or polenta. As with soups, a braised meat dish like this always tastes better when made a day ahead. *–Michael*

serves 4

2 pieces beef short ribs (4 bones)
Salt and pepper
2 tbsp/25 mL vegetable oil
2 cups/500 mL mixed diced celery,
     carrots, and onion
5 cloves garlic, slivered
1 bay leaf
2 sprigs thyme
3 tbsp/45 mL tomato paste
4 cups/1 L full-bodied red wine
2 cups/500 mL beef stock
1 cup/250 mL diced canned tomatoes
1 tbsp/15 mL chopped chipotle
     peppers in adobo

- Preheat the oven to 350°F (180° C).

- Season the ribs with salt and pepper. Heat the oil in a Dutch oven over medium-high heat and sear the ribs until golden brown. Add the celery, carrots, onions, garlic, bay leaf, and thyme. Sauté over medium-high heat for 4 to 6 minutes. Stir in the tomato paste and cook for 3 to 4 minutes, stirring often. Add the wine, stock, tomatoes, and chipotle peppers. Season with salt and pepper and simmer for 2 to 3 minutes. Skim any fat that has risen and reduce the heat to low.

- Partially cover the pot and slowly simmer for 2½ to 3 hours, turning the ribs 2 or 3 times during cooking. When the meat pulls away from the bone, they are done. Remove from the heat and cool for 20 minutes. Gently lift out the ribs.

- Adjust the sauce by checking the seasoning and the consistency. If it is too thick, add a splash more broth or water; if it is too thin, return it to the heat and simmer until it's thick enough to coat the back of a spoon.

- Add the ribs back to the sauce to reheat.

striploin salad Thai-Cremona style

My mother had a series of recipes that she rotated through. Since Sunday lunch was a big production, we always had lots of leftovers, most of them deliberate. The best pieces of meat were reserved for the beef salad, a family favourite. Fast forward to my arrival in Canada. A friend introduced me to Thai beef salad, thinking I would be surprised by it. I was—but by its similarities to my mother's recipe, not by its strangeness. *–Massimo*

serves 4

1 lb/500 g striploin steak, trimmed
   of fat
Salt and pepper
1 medium onion, thinly sliced
½ red pepper, thinly sliced
½ yellow pepper, thinly sliced
2 cups/500 mL halved grape tomatoes
1 bunch cilantro or Italian parsley,
   chopped
1 clove garlic, chopped
1 anchovy, chopped
Juice of 1 lime
Juice of 1 lemon
Leaf lettuce, for garnish
Tomato slices, for garnish

- Season the steak with salt and pepper and grill to medium rare. Wrap in foil and set aside to cool completely.
- In a bowl, combine the onions, peppers, and tomatoes with the cilantro, garlic, anchovy, lemon and lime juices, and olive oil as needed. Let sit for about 30 minutes.
- Slice the beef thinly and mix with the remaining ingredients. Serve over tender leaf lettuce with slices of tomato and crusty bread on the side.

Jason's ultimate burger

Many people do not realize that the secret to keeping a burger moist while cooking is adding some kind of fat to it. In this case, I use lean beef and the fat from the bacon. When it comes to taste, bacon fat trumps beef fat any day. *–Jason*

serves 8

for the burgers:

3 lbs/1.5 kg lean ground beef

2 cups/500 mL diced aged cheddar cheese

½ cup/125 mL finely chopped herbs

¼ cup/50 mL chopped onion

¼ cup/50 mL hoisin sauce

2 tbsp/25 mL finely chopped garlic

1 tbsp/15 mL Worcestershire sauce

2 cups/500 mL chopped bacon

2 eggs

½ cup/125 mL bread crumbs

3 tsp/15 mL salt

3 tsp/15 mL ground white pepper

for the glaze:

½ cup/125 mL barbecue sauce

¼ cup/50 mL hoisin sauce

2 tbsp/25 mL honey

1 tsp/5 mL ground cinnamon

for the assembly:

8 burger buns

¼ cup/60 mL grape mustard (or Dijon)

16 leaves watercress

16 slices tomato

8 slices red onion

burgers: In a large mixing bowl, combine the ground beef, cheddar, herbs, onions, hoisin, garlic, and Worcestershire.

- Sauté the bacon over medium heat until cooked through. Add the warm bacon, including the fat, to the beef mixture. Stir in the eggs, bread crumbs, salt, and pepper. Once it's well combined, form the mixture into eight evenly sized burgers and chill.

glaze: Combine the barbecue sauce with the hoisin, honey, and cinnamon.

assembly: Cook the burgers on a very hot grill, brushing with the glaze each time they are turned. Warm the buns on the side or on the top rack. Once the burgers are cooked through, remove from the grill and brush once more with the glaze.

- Spread the mustard on the bottom layer of each bun.
- Add the burger, watercress, sliced tomato, and onion; cap with the bun top.

cook's note: The chopped herbs can be any mix of your favourite seasonings. I like tarragon, parsley, and chives.

classic tourtière

Tourtière is a French-Canadian meat pie. There are endless variations on the recipe, all built on a blend of meat, poultry, and seasonings—feel free to tweak this to your own taste. It's traditionally served at Christmastime, with chutney or a savoury ketchup, but it makes a delicious meal any time of year. I like to make a batch and freeze them. –*Michael*

makes 12 to 14 mini tourtières

2 tbsp/25 mL butter
4 oz/125 g ground pork
4 oz/125 g ground beef
8 oz/250 g ground duck, venison, quail,
    or any other meat of your choice
¾ cup/175 mL minced onions
1 clove garlic, crushed
¾ tsp/3 mL salt
¼ tsp/1 mL pepper
¼ tsp/1 mL allspice
1 tbsp/15 mL chopped parsley
1 tbsp/15 mL chopped thyme leaves
⅔ cup/150 mL beef stock
2 tbsp/25 mL Worcestershire sauce
1 tbsp/15 mL cognac
1 tbsp/15 mL bread crumbs
1 sheet puff pastry, rolled ⅛ inch/
    2.5 mm thick
1 egg whisked with 1 tbsp/15 mL milk

- Preheat the oven to 375°F (190°C).

- Heat the butter in a large skillet over medium-high heat. Brown the meat, in batches, if necessary, so it doesn't stew. Add the onions, garlic, salt, pepper, allspice, parsley, and thyme. Cook for 5 to 10 minutes on medium-low heat, until the onions are tender. Add the stock, Worcestershire sauce, and cognac. Simmer over low heat for 20 to 30 minutes, reducing to a glaze.
- Remove from the heat and stir in the bread crumbs. Refrigerate for at least 1 hour. Once cooled, divide the mixture into 12 equal balls and set aside.
- While the tourtière mixture is cooling, place the sheet of puff pastry on a floured surface. Using a 4- to 5-inch (10 to 12.5 cm) cutter, cut out 12 circles. Pinch each circle with your thumb and index finger to stretch the pastry slightly. Place a scoop of the meat mixture in the centre of each circle, leaving a small edge. Pull the pastry edges into the centre of the meat so the mixture is completely covered and you have a puck-shaped pie approximately 3 inches (7.5 cm) in diameter. Brush the edges lightly with the egg wash and pinch to close.
- Chill the tourtières for 30 minutes in the refrigerator.
- Place the tourtières on a lightly greased baking sheet with the pinched-together edges hidden underneath. Brush each pie again with the egg wash and bake them in the oven for 15 to 20 minutes, until golden brown.

prosciutto and mushroom beef Wellington

When I was a kid, we always had beef Wellington at Christmas dinner. My grandmother served roasted lamb on the big occasions, so I guess this was my mom's way of being experimental and individual. I still like to cook beef Wellington, but I like to play around with the traditional ingredients. In this version, I love the flavour the prosciutto gives the beef as it cooks. *–Jason*

serves 6

1 tbsp/15 mL butter
½ cup/125 mL sliced shallots
1 tbsp/15 mL chopped garlic
4 cups/1 L chopped mushrooms
    (shiitake, oyster, chanterelle)
1 tbsp/15 mL chopped tarragon
Salt and pepper
1 tbsp/15 mL grapeseed oil
1 lb/500 g beef tenderloin
8 slices prosciutto
1 sheet puff pastry, rolled to a thin
    rectangle
5 egg yolks, lightly whisked

- Preheat the oven to 400°F (200°C).

- Melt the butter in a large skillet over medium-high heat. Add the shallots, garlic, and mushrooms; cook until browned. Add the tarragon and season with salt and pepper, then transfer to a bowl with a slotted spoon to cool.
- Heat the oil in the skillet over high heat. Sear the beef until brown on all sides. Season with salt and pepper, then set aside to cool.
- Place a large piece of plastic wrap on the counter. In the centre, lay out two rows of prosciutto, cover them with the cooked mushroom mixture, and top with the beef. Using the plastic wrap, roll the prosciutto around the mushrooms and beef to create a cylinder. Wrap and chill for 1 hour in the refrigerator.
- Lay the pastry flat on the counter. Remove the plastic from the wrapped beef and place the beef in the centre of the pastry. Brush the edges of the pastry with the egg and roll it around the beef, pinching the edges together, then fold the ends underneath. Brush the outside of the pastry with the remaining egg and chill in the refrigerator.
- Roast the beef on a large baking pan for approximately 25 minutes. Remove and let rest for 5 minutes before slicing.

grilled flatiron steak
with garlic cream and Brussels sprouts

If steaks are out of your budget, try flatiron or skirt steaks: they're very tender, and in my opinion they're more flavourful. Making a cream out of garlic is a great technique; we often do it with our famous Kobe flatiron steak, and it is always a popular addition. —*Massimo*

serves 4

for the steak:
2 lb/1 kg flatiron beef, cut into
    4 8 oz/250 g portions
Salt and pepper
2 tbsp/25 mL butter, softened

for the garlic cream:
8 cloves garlic
1 sprig thyme
1 cup/250 mL homogenized milk
    (more if needed)
4 slices white bread, crusts removed,
    cubed

for the squash chips:
1 buttercup squash,
    peeled and thinly sliced
Salt and pepper
Granulated sugar
2 tbsp/25 mL butter, softened

for the Brussels sprouts:
2 tbsp/25 mL butter
12 Brussels sprouts,
    separated into leaves

- Preheat the oven to 375°F (190°C).

steak: Season the beef with salt and pepper and spread with a thin layer of butter.
- Preheat a grill pan on high heat and sear the beef for approximately 3 minutes per side. Wrap in foil and set aside for 5 minutes.

garlic cream: Combine the garlic, thyme, and milk in a saucepan and cook over medium-high heat until the garlic is tender. Add the bread and cook for 10 more minutes. Add additional milk, if necessary, to smooth the mixture.
- Using a stick blender, emulsify well and season to taste. Set aside.

squash chips: Season the squash with salt, pepper, and a sprinkle of sugar. Rub with the butter and place on a parchment−lined baking sheet. Bake in the oven, turning occasionally, until the squash is golden. Remove and let cool−don't worry if it's not crisp, since that will happen as it cools.

Brussels sprouts: Melt the butter in a skillet over medium-high heat and sauté the leaves for 1 to 2 minutes. Set aside.

assembly: Place some garlic cream on a plate and drag it to form a line.
- Scatter the squash chips over the cream in a criss-cross pattern and sprinkle the Brussels sprouts leaves over top. Slice the beef thinly, place over the sprouts, and drizzle with olive oil.

pan-roasted prime rib with sticky onion gravy

Nothing very fancy here—just straightforward carnivorous goodness. Roasted or mashed potatoes, green beans, or a simple, crisp salad are delicious accompaniments. —Michael

serves 4

4   1 lb/500 g prime ribs (have your
      butcher trim and tie them)
Salt and pepper
1 tbsp/15 mL olive oil
6 large onions, thinly sliced
1 clove garlic, minced
1 sprig thyme, chopped
¼ cup/50 mL balsamic vinegar
1 cup/250 mL beef broth
1 tsp/5 mL honey
1 tbsp/15 mL butter
4 tsp/20 mL chopped chives

- Season the meat well with salt and pepper. Heat the oil in a large pan over medium-high heat and sear the beef on all sides until golden brown.
- Roast in the oven for 6 to 8 minutes (for medium-rare), or until the beef is done to your liking. Remove it from the pan and cover it with foil to keep warm.
- Add the onions to the pan and cook vigorously over medium-high heat, stirring and turning to prevent them from sticking or burning, until golden brown.
- Add the garlic and thyme and continue to cook for 15 to 18 minutes.
- Stir in the vinegar, a splash of broth, and the honey. Simmer until the onions are dark and rich in colour (the flavour will be mild and sweet but acidic).
- Add just enough broth to create a little pan gravy, whisking in the butter just before serving. Place one prime rib on each plate, spoon over a healthy amount of the sticky onion gravy, and sprinkle with chopped chives.

beef tenderloin
with Gorgonzola, roasted onions, and pancetta

This recipe might seem as if it came out of a roadhouse, but if flavour is what you are after, then it's for you. I included this recipe on the menu of Fraticelli, the Italian concept restaurant I had the pleasure to help open, and it has been a runaway success. *–Massimo*

serves 4

4 8 oz/250 g beef tenderloins
Salt and pepper
¼ cup/50 mL butter
¼ cup/50 mL olive oil
1 sprig rosemary
1 sprig sage
1 sprig thyme
3 tbsp/45 mL chopped shallots
2 garlic cloves, lightly crushed
½ cup/125 mL red wine
2 tbsp/25 mL balsamic vinegar
4 oz/125 g Gorgonzola cheese
2 tbsp/25 mL mascarpone cheese
2 tbsp/25 mL sour cream
1 cup/250 mL thinly sliced onions
1 cup/250 mL diced pancetta,
    ½-inch/1 cm cubes

- Season the beef with salt and pepper. Heat 1 tbsp (15 mL) of the butter and half the oil in a skillet over medium-high heat along with the rosemary, sage, and thyme. Sear the beef to your preferred doneness. Remove from the pan, wrap in foil, and set aside to keep warm.
- Add the shallots and garlic to the pan and cook until they're translucent. Pour in the wine and reduce until slightly creamy. Add the balsamic and reduce again until creamy. Stir in 1 tbsp (15 mL) of the butter, and when it melts, remove the pan from the heat. Strain the sauce to remove all solids.
- Blend the Gorgonzola, mascarpone, and sour cream in a food processor. Season with salt and pepper to taste, and set aside.
- In a skillet, heat the remaining 2 tbsp (25 mL) of the butter and oil over medium-low heat. Add the onions and pancetta and cook slowly until the onions are completely caramelized.
- Place one tenderloin on each plate and cover with the onion and pancetta mixture. Top with a scoop of the Gorgonzola mixture and allow the cheese to melt.

8: a bit on the side

sautéed leaves with raisins and pine nuts

Throughout the year you can easily find some sort of leafy vegetable that's perfect for a quick sautéed side dish to go with meat or fish. I always have a random assortment on hand at Mistura: the waiters are often asked for sautéed spinach or rapini by guests who need a green fix. –*Massimo*

serves 6

1 bunch broccolini, about 6 stems
8 oz/250 g green beans
2 cups/500 mL coarsely chopped
    Swiss chard leaves, stems reserved
2 tbsp/25 mL olive oil
1 cup/250 mL sliced leeks
2 garlic cloves, sliced
3 tbsp/45 mL pine nuts
3 tbsp/45 mL sultana raisins
2 cups/500 mL coarsely chopped
    escarole leaves
2 cups/500 mL spinach leaves
    (preferably curly)
Salt and pepper

- Blanch the broccolini in salted water until cooked but still crisp, then drain and shock in cold water. Set aside. Repeat the process with the green beans.
- Boil the chard stems in salted, acidulated water (put a slice of lemon in it) until soft, then cool under running water. Drain and set aside.
- Heat the olive oil in a sauté pan on medium-high heat. Sauté the leeks and garlic for 2 minutes. Before they burn, add the pine nuts and raisins and increase the heat to high. Toss in the leafy greens starting with the chard leaves. Cook for 1 minute, then add the escarole, spinach, green beans, broccolini, and chard stems. Season with salt and pepper and serve immediately.

bubble and squeak

I grew up in a family of four, but my mother always cooked for 10 (or so it seemed). Maybe this is why I've never been a fan of leftovers and have always looked for ways to reinvent them. I love the idea of taking a vegetable and some meat and making this nice little side dish. Don't get rid of any of the rendered bacon fat: that's where a big part of the flavour comes from. *–Jason*

serves 4

1 cup/250 mL diced bacon
½ cup/125 mL sliced shallots
2 cups/500 mL diced Yukon Gold
   potatoes, cooked
2 tbsp/25 mL butter
3 cups/750 mL sliced raw Brussels
   sprouts (or leftover cooked)
¼ cup/50 mL chicken stock
1 tsp/5 mL nutmeg
Salt and pepper

- Fry the bacon in a pan over high heat. Add the shallots and sauté until golden, then toss in the potatoes and butter. When the potatoes are warmed through, add the Brussels sprouts, chicken stock, and nutmeg. Cook for 2 minutes, then season with salt and pepper.

all peas in all shapes

Green peas are one of the great gifts of spring and are simply delicious with butter.
If you've ever picked your own or bought them directly from a farm, you know how
wonderful they are fresh. But you can catch some of that pleasure year-round: good
quality frozen peas are frozen right after they're picked, retaining all their sweetness and
freshness. They are often better than "fresh" peas that have taken a couple of days to get
to market. This is the one frozen food that I'm happy to include in my diet. *–Massimo*

serves 4

2 tbsp/25 mL butter
1 tbsp/15 mL olive oil
2 tbsp/25 mL finely sliced shallots
2 cloves garlic, thinly sliced
1 cup/250 mL green peas
1 cup/250 mL thinly sliced snow peas
1 cup/250 mL split sugar snap peas
    (split lengthwise to reveal the peas)
2 cups/500 mL pea shoots
Salt and pepper

• Heat the butter and olive oil in a skillet over high heat.
Sauté the shallots and the garlic until translucent. Add
the green peas and cook for 3 minutes, then add the snow
peas and sugar snaps and cook for 1 minute more. Toss in
the pea shoots to wilt. Season with salt and pepper.

butternut squash, chestnut, and sage ratatouille

I really like ratatouille. I think it's a great dish, even if it might seem rather rustic and déclassé, too much of a peasant food. I think it's a great way to play around with vegetables, especially in the winter when the only local produce available is squash. You're really forced to think of ways to make it good. The pumpkin seeds are a fun addition, giving the dish another layer of texture and flavour. *–Jason*

serves 4

1 tbsp/15 mL butter
2 cups/500 mL diced blanched
    butternut squash
½ cup/125 mL sliced shallots
1 clove garlic, thinly sliced
2 cups/500 mL seeded diced
    tomatoes
1 cup/250 mL cooked and diced
    chestnuts
½ cup/125 mL toasted pumpkin seeds
¼ cup/50 icewine (or substitute apple
    cider)
½ cup/125 mL beef stock
¼ cup/50 mL sage leaves
Salt and pepper

- Melt the butter in a saucepan over medium-high heat. Sauté the squash, shallots, and garlic for 1 minute. Add the tomatoes, chestnuts, pumpkin seeds, and icewine. When warmed through, add the beef stock and sage. Bring to a simmer, season with salt and pepper and serve.

mixed mushroom gratin

This is a delicious and easy recipe—it's one of those dishes that tastes much fancier than it is. And it's incredibly flexible: you can serve it over a spinach salad, as a side dish with grilled meat, or on its own as an appetizer. –*Michael*

serves 4

1 tbsp/15 mL olive oil

½ cup/125 mL thinly sliced shallots

3 cloves garlic, slivered

4 cups/1 L sliced mixed mushrooms
   (oyster, shiitake, button, etc)

Salt and pepper

¼ cup/50 mL whipping (35%) cream

¼ cup/50 mL grated Parmesan
   cheese

¼ cup/50 mL panko bread crumbs

½ tsp/2 mL chopped thyme leaves

- Heat the olive oil in a sauté pan over medium heat. Sauté the shallots and garlic until light golden brown, about 5 minutes. Add the mushrooms and increase the heat to high. Sauté quickly, seasoning with salt and pepper. Pour in the cream and reduce by half.
- Transfer the mushrooms to an oven-proof serving dish. Combine the Parmesan cheese, panko crumbs, and thyme; sprinkle over the mushrooms.
- Place under a preheated broiler until the crust becomes light golden brown. Serve immediately.

poutine with cured bacon and chorizo

I first put poutine on the menu some years ago and was about to take it off when the trend hit, so I decided to wait. Now I'm not able to—any time I've tried, the complaints have been loud and endless. Some version of it is always on our menu. The icing sugar is my secret ingredient: it gives a very subtle sweetness to the fries and makes them nice and crisp. *–Jason*

serves 4

6 Yukon Gold potatoes
2 tbsp/25 mL thyme leaves
2 tsp/10 mL icing sugar
2 tsp/10 mL sea salt
1 cup/250 mL cheese curds
1 cup/250 mL grated aged cheddar
    cheese
1 cup/250 mL diced bacon
1 chorizo sausage, diced
1 tbsp/15 mL cracked black pepper
¾ cup/175 mL beef gravy

- Preheat a deep fryer to 140°F (60°C).

- Cut the potatoes into French fries (skin on or off—it's your choice). Cook the fries in the deep fryer for 3 to 4 minutes, until just cooked but not golden. Spread on a baking tray and cool in the refrigerator.
- Turn the deep fryer up to 180°F (85°C) and return the chilled fries to the oil. Crisp the fries until golden brown then remove and dry on paper towels. Dust with the thyme, icing sugar, and sea salt.
- Mix the fries with the cheese curds, cheddar, bacon, and chorizo and distribute among four bowls. Add the pepper to the gravy and warm through.
- Just before serving, pour the black pepper gravy over the fries, allowing the heat of the gravy to melt the cheese.

wild rice and forest mushroom risotto

One of my great discoveries when I moved to Canada was all the varieties of wild rice available. If you want me to get excited, show me some rice: the Padania Valley, where I grew up, is a major rice-growing area and we ate it every day. Technically, wild rice isn't rice at all—it's a long-grain marsh grass somewhat akin to wheat. But it cooks like rice, and its flavour and texture are fabulous, so who cares? *—Massimo*

serves 5

¾ cup/175 g wild rice
1 tbsp/15 mL olive oil
3 tbsp/45 mL butter
3 tbsp/45 mL chopped onions
1 tbsp/15 mL chopped wild leeks
2½ cups/625 mL chopped mixed
    forest mushrooms (morel, trumpet,
    chanterelle, porcini)
1½ cups/300 g carnaroli rice
¾ cup/175 mL white wine
10 cups/2.5 L chicken stock
¼ cup/50 mL grated Parmigiano-
    Reggiano cheese

- Soak the wild rice overnight in room-temperature water. Cook for 15 minutes in salted, boiling water, then drain and set aside.
- Heat the oil and 1 tbsp (15 mL) of the butter in a heavy-bottomed pot. Sauté the onions and the wild leeks for 3 minutes, until translucent. Add the mushrooms and cook for 3 minutes. Add the carnaroli and wild rice and heat for 1 minute, stirring gently to prevent burning. Pour in the wine, let it evaporate completely, then add two ladles of stock.
- Simmer gently, stirring occasionally to prevent sticking, and adding stock as needed to keep the rice moist.
- It will take about 18 minutes for this rice to cook, so keep your timer in sight and continue to add stock as required until the rice is cooked.
- When finished, the risotto should be runny but not liquid.
- Add the remaining butter and the cheese, mixing vigorously to draw in some air and make it fluffy.

wild rice and Gruyère risotto

This isn't actually a "risotto" recipe, since it doesn't use arborio rice and there's no slow, high-maintenance cooking. It's a kind of cheater risotto. But the cheese, butter, and stock all melt together to give a flavourful creaminess that's very convincing. *–Jason*

serves 4

3 tbsp/45 mL butter
¼ cup/50 mL sliced shallots
1 tbsp/15 mL chopped garlic
1 cup/250 mL chopped mushrooms
1 cup/250 mL cooked long grain rice
1 cup/250 mL cooked wild rice
1 cup/250 mL chicken stock
½ cup/125 mL grated Gruyère cheese
¼ cup/50 mL grated Parmesan
    cheese
Salt and pepper
¼ cup/50 mL chopped parsley

- Melt 1 tbsp (15 mL) of the butter in a saucepan over medium-high heat. Add the shallots and garlic and sauté for 1 minute. Add the mushrooms and sauté for 2 minutes. Stir in the long grain and wild rice and the chicken stock. Warm through, then add the remaining butter. When the butter is melted, add the Gruyère and Parmesan.
- Remove from the heat, season with salt and pepper, and garnish with the parsley. Serve immediately.

white beans all'uccelletto

Beans are good for so many reasons, not the least their versatility. They're widely used in Italian kitchens for soups, salads, stews, side dishes—even, lately, in terrines and ice cream. The key seasoning here is sage, which is where the name comes from. "Uccelletto" means "little bird," and by Tuscan tradition, birds *must* be cooked with sage. Therefore, if you cook beans with sage, they're "beans in the manner of birds." *–Massimo*

serves 4

3 tbsp/45 mL olive oil
2 cloves garlic, minced
1 tbsp/15 mL chopped sage
½ cup/125 mL diced tomatoes, peeled
   and seeded
2 cups/500 mL cooked cannellini
   beans
Salt and pepper

- Heat the oil in a saucepan over medium-high heat. Sauté the garlic and sage just until the garlic begins to brown.
- Add the tomatoes, then reduce the heat to medium and simmer for 10 minutes.
- Stir in the beans, reduce heat to low, and cook slowly for 10 minutes. Season to taste with salt and pepper.

Parmigiano tuiles

At Mistura, we use Parmigiano tuiles in many ways: as snacks with apéritifs, as vessels for pasta and risotto, as garnishes for salads. We have guests who eat piles of them at once. Often I make them just by melting the cheese on its own in a non-stick skillet. Always use a young cheese and be sure to grate from the centre where there's more moisture. *–Massimo*

makes about 12 tuiles

1 large baking potato
¼ cup/50 mL grated Parmigiano-
   Reggiano cheese, ideally 18 to 24
   months old
2 tbsp/25 mL butter

- Boil the potato in salted water until fork tender, then cool it completely.
- Peel the potato and shred it as finely as possible, spreading it on a tray. Sprinkle the cheese over the potato and let it rest it for a minute before stirring to fluff it up. If the mixture seems too wet, add more cheese. Set aside.
- Heat a non-stick skillet over medium heat, then brush some butter on the bottom of the pan. Making one at a time, sprinkle about ¼ cup (50 mL) of the potato-cheese mixture into the pan and gently press it down to form a thin tuile. Cook the tuile on one side until golden, then turn it over and continue to cook until crispy.

cook's note: Store the tuiles in a cool, dry place. They'll keep for two or three days.

9: sweet talk

icewine marshmallows

About three years ago, one of my chefs asked me how marshmallows are made. I had no idea, but since then Peller has become known for its icewine-roasted marshmallows, prepared on our open firepits and served with a glass of cabernet franc icewine. This year alone, over the three-week Icewine Festival, we went through 3,000 marshmallows! It is always good to ask questions, and it's even more fun learning the answers. *–Jason*

makes 40 marshmallows

¾ cup/175 mL cold water
3 pkg unflavoured gelatin
2 tbsp/25 mL icewine reduction
2 cups/500 mL granulated sugar
⅔ cup/150 mL corn syrup
¼ tsp/1 mL salt
1 vanilla bean
Icing sugar for dusting

- Pour ½ cup (125 mL) of the cold water and the gelatin into the bowl of a stand mixer and let sit for 10 minutes.
- Meanwhile, mix the remaining water, the icewine reduction, sugar, and corn syrup in a pot. Bring to a boil and simmer for 1 minute.
- Remove from the heat and add to the mixing bowl with the water and gelatin. Add the salt and whisk on high for 8 minutes. Add the seeds from the vanilla bean and whisk for another 2 minutes on low, just enough to blend.
- Line a 9-inch (22.5 cm) square cake pan with plastic wrap and spray with non-stick coating. Pour the mixture into the pan and let it set in a cool, dry area (but not the refrigerator).
- Once the marshmallows are firm, cut into forty 1-inch (2.5 cm) squares and dust with icing sugar.

cook's note: To make the icewine reduction, simmer 1 cup (250 mL) of icewine down to 2 tbsp (25 mL). You can also use a late-harvest wine, which lacks a little of the richness of icewine but is much cheaper.

lemon posset

Originally, in the Middle Ages, a posset was a therapeutic drink made from hot, spiced milk and honey spiked with ale or wine. It was only later that it evolved into a thickened cream dessert. I was given this recipe by celebrity chef Annabel Langbein on my visit to New Zealand. It's one of the quickest and easiest dessert recipes ever. It reminds me of crème brûlée without the brûlée–delicate, soft, creamy, and refreshing, but very intense in flavour. –*Michael*

serves 6

2¼ cups/550 mL whipping (35%) cream
⅔ cup/150 mL granulated sugar
¼ cup/50 mL lemon juice, strained
Fresh strawberries or blackberries, for garnish
Sprig of mint, for garnish
Icing sugar, for garnish

- In a medium pot, combine the cream and sugar and bring them to a simmer, stirring until the sugar has dissolved. Remove from the heat and stir in the lemon juice.
- Pour the mixture into six ramekins or bowls and refrigerate for at least 4 hours.
- Garnish with fresh berries, a sprig of mint, and a dusting of icing sugar.

chocolate and blueberry crêpes

Crêpes are very popular in Northern Italy, as a street food and in restaurants, many of which offer both sweet and savoury versions. The crêperie in the resort town of Punta Ala in Tuscany was a great place to take dates and was a favourite destination of mine when I was young and carefree. *–Massimo*

serves 4

for the crêpes:
3 eggs
Pinch salt
¼ cup/50 mL butter, melted
1 cup/250 mL all-purpose flour
1¼ cups/300 mL milk

for the blueberries:
4 cups/1 L wild blueberries
1 cup/250 mL granulated sugar
Zest of 1 lemon
Juice of ½ lemon

for the ganache:
¾ cup/175 mL whipping (35%) cream
8 oz/250 g bittersweet chocolate,
    cut in small pieces
2 tbsp/25 mL butter
1 tbsp/15 mL cognac
Pinch salt

- Preheat the oven to 350°F (180°C).

crêpes: Crack the eggs in a bowl. Add the salt and melted butter and mix well. Add the flour and mix well, then stir in the milk. Rest the batter in the refrigerator for 2 to 3 hours.
- Preheat a crêpe pan and grease it lightly with butter. Coat the bottom very thinly with batter, about ½ oz (15 mL), and cook. Flip the crêpe and cook the other side, being careful not to over-colour. Repeat.

blueberries: Combine the blueberries, sugar, lemon zest, and juice. Cook over medium heat until dense and creamy. Set aside.

ganache: Boil the cream and pour it over the chocolate in a bowl. Stir in the butter, cognac, and salt; mix well and set aside to cool.

assembly: Spread each crêpe with a thin layer of chocolate and spoon some blueberry mixture on top. Roll up the crêpe and heat it in the oven for 3 minutes, just long enough to reheat. Serve two per person with vanilla ice cream and extra dollops of blueberry sauce.

passion fruit curd tart

My brother lives in Australia, and a couple of years ago I visited him there. Most mornings we'd have fresh passion fruit in Greek-style yogurt for breakfast. I've craved passion fruit ever since and look for ways to sneak it into various recipes, such as this takeoff on lemon tart. *–Michael*

serves 6

1 cup/250 mL all-purpose flour
Pinch salt
½ cup/125 mL unsalted butter, chilled and cut into cubes
1 vanilla bean
2 tbsp/25 mL icing sugar
Zest of 1 lemon
5 egg yolks
Ice water
1 beaten egg white, for brushing
10 wrinkly passion fruit
2 eggs
½ cup/125 mL granulated sugar (or more to taste)
½ cup/125 mL unsalted butter
Crème fraîche, for garnish (or whipped cream)
Fresh mint, for garnish
Icing sugar, for garnish

- Preheat the oven to 350°F (180°C).

- Combine the flour and salt in a bowl. Rub in the butter until the mixture resembles fine bread crumbs.
- Cut the vanilla bean in half lengthwise and scrape out the seeds. Add three seeds to the bowl and stir in the icing sugar and lemon zest. Add two of the egg yolks and enough ice water to bring the mixture together into a smooth dough.
- Roll out the pastry to line an 8-inch (20 cm) tart tin. Chill for 30 to 45 minutes.
- Bake blind for 15 minutes, then remove the weights and paper. Prick the bottom and the sides of the tart shell; brush with egg white.
- Return to the oven for 10 minutes, or until the pastry is firm and pale gold in colour. Remove and cool.
- In a small saucepan, scoop out the flesh of the passion fruit and heat very gently on low heat, just enough to warm it without cooking. Using a sieve, strain the fruit very thoroughly into a bowl to extract as much juice as possible. Reserve the seeds.

- Beat the two whole eggs and three remaining egg yolks with sugar. Melt the remaining butter in a pan on low heat and stir in the passion fruit juice, followed by the egg mixture. Continue to cook, stirring constantly, for 6 to 8 minutes until it thickens. Remove from the heat and stir in 1 tbsp (15 mL) of the reserved seeds.
- Pour the passion fruit curd into the cooled tart shell and let set for 2 to 3 hours.
- To serve, garnish with a scoop of crème fraîche and top with a sprig of mint. Dust with icing sugar and serve.

cook's note: To blind bake the pastry, first prick it all over to prevent it from blistering and rising. Line it with parchment paper, then fill it with dried beans, clean pebbles, or pie weights. Remove the weights and paper a few minutes before the baking time is up to allow the crust to brown.

Mom's English trifle

I ate a lot of trifle as a kid; it was a staple in our house (Mom always made one with alcohol and one without), so I never really thought of it as something to make as a chef—it was "home cooking." But one day, on the TV show, we were talking about classics our moms had made, and I decided to make one. It was a lot of fun and brought back lots of memories—and it was really tasty! *–Jason*

serves 12 to 16

1 angel food cake (or any sponge cake)
1 cup/250 mL raspberry jam
¼ cup/50 mL granulated sugar
1 cup/250 mL blackberries
2 cups/500 mL strawberries
1 cup/250 mL raspberries
1½ cups/375 mL water
1 cup/250 mL orange juice
1 pkg unflavoured gelatin
2 cups/500 mL custard
2 cups/500 mL whipping (35%) cream, whipped
½ cup/125 mL grated chocolate

- Cut the cake into 1-inch (2.5 cm) slices. Layer the pieces on the bottom and halfway up the sides of a large glass bowl. Spread the jam over the cake.
- In a separate bowl, mix the sugar and berries; set aside. Warm the water and orange juice in a pot over high heat. Whisk in the gelatin to dissolve it, then pour the liquid over the berries and sugar. Combine thoroughly, then drizzle it over the cake and place the bowl in the refrigerator.
- When the berries and gelatin have set, layer the custard over top and return the trifle to the refrigerator to firm up.
- Finish with the whipped cream and grated chocolate.

chocolate and pistachio paté

I love this dish. Chefs go through phases, and for a while mine was paté and terrines in all forms: rabbit, foie gras, what have you. I decided to play around with a sweet one and came up with this. It's like a Toblerone bar but way better. –*Jason*

makes 12 to16 slices

for the white chocolate paté:
- 1¼ cups/300 mL white chocolate
- ½ cup/125 mL condensed milk
- ¼ cup/50 mL chopped dried cherries

for the dark chocolate paté:
- 3½ cups/875 mL dark chocolate
- 1½ cups/375 mL condensed milk
- ¾ cup/175 mL chopped toasted pistachios
- 1 tbsp/15 mL vidal icewine (or other late-harvest white)

white chocolate paté (must be made first): Line a triangular paté mould with waxed paper. Melt the white chocolate in a bowl over a pot of simmering water.
- Stir in the condensed milk and dried cherries. Pour the mixture into the mould and chill in the refrigerator until firm. Remove from the mould and set aside.

dark chocolate paté: Clean the paté mould and again line with waxed paper.
- Melt the dark chocolate in a bowl over a pot of simmering water.
- Stir in the condensed milk, pistachios, and icewine. Pour three quarters of the mixture into the mould.
- Let sit for 2 to 3 minutes, then press the white chocolate paté into the centre of the dark chocolate. Pour in the remaining dark chocolate to cover the white chocolate. Refrigerate until firm.

chocolate sauce

This is a simple and versatile recipe that goes with many desserts—like the panna cotta and cheesecake that follow. *–Massimo*

makes about 3 cups

5 oz/150 g dark chocolate, best quality possible
¼ cup/50 mL light corn syrup
1 tsp/5 mL vanilla extract
¾ cup/175 mL water
½ cup/125 mL granulated sugar
2 tbsp/25 mL cocoa powder

- Cut the chocolate into small pieces and place in a bowl with the corn syrup and vanilla.
- Combine the water and sugar in a saucepan and bring to a boil. Remove from the heat and slowly whisk in the cocoa powder, then pour over the chocolate and syrup. Mix until all the ingredients have dissolved completely and set aside to cool.

chestnut and chocolate panna cotta

Panna cotta is a relatively new dessert, having appeared in the last 20 years or so, and it happens to be one of my favourite ways to end a meal. I don't usually eat dessert: I enjoy the savoury part of the meal more than the sweet, so something light with a lot of flavour and some fruit is what I usually go for. Try this recipe in the fall when chestnuts are plentiful and fresh berries are scarce. *–Massimo*

serves 4

3 sheets of gelatin (or 1 tsp/5 mL gelatin powder)

2 cups/500 mL whipping (35%) cream

½ cup/125 mL granulated sugar

2 tbsp/25 mL bittersweet chocolate chips

2 tbsp/25 mL Crème de Cacao liqueur

⅔ cup/150 mL puréed chestnuts

1 tbsp/15 mL sour cream

Chocolate sauce

Whipped cream, for garnish

- Soak the gelatin sheets in cold water to soften them.
- Boil half the cream with the sugar and remove from the heat when the sugar has dissolved.
- Strain the gelatin and add it to the cream, stirring well to melt it. Add the chocolate chips and the liqueur and combine thoroughly. Add the chestnut purée and mix until smooth, then set aside to cool.
- Whip the remaining cream with the sour cream and fold it into the panna cotta mixture just as it begins to solidify. Pour the panna cotta into four ramekins and refrigerate for at least 1 hour.
- Unmould and serve with chocolate sauce and whipped cream.

pistachio cheesecake

Classic New York–style cheesecake is hard to find in Italy, but I know this one would be very popular. The sweet nuttiness of the pistachio and the creaminess of the cheese go together so well. To make good cheesecake, you must use the best quality cheese you can find. Cook it just long enough that the centre is barely set, then turn the oven off, open the door slightly, and let the cheesecake rest and settle for at least one hour. –*Massimo*

serves 8

2 lbs/1 kg cream cheese, softened to room temperature
1¾ cups/425 mL granulated sugar
2 tbsp/25 mL lemon juice
¼ cup/50 mL all-purpose flour
½ tsp/2 mL salt
8 eggs
2 cups/500 mL homogenized milk
⅓ cup/75 mL pistachio paste
1 disc sponge cake, 1 inch/2.5 cm thick, 10 inches/25 cm in diameter (or substitute graham cracker crumbs)

- Preheat the oven to 350°F (180°C).

- Using an electric mixer, whip the cheese with the sugar at medium speed until creamy. Add the lemon juice and mix slowly. Sift in the flour and continue to mix slowly. Add the salt and then the eggs, one at a time, and continue to mix slowly. Add the milk and the pistachio paste and combine thoroughly.
- Line the bottom of a 10-inch (25 cm) springform pan with a disc of sponge cake and pour in the cream cheese mixture.
- Bake for about 45 minutes or until the middle of the cake has set. Do not over-bake: the cheesecake should be wobbly, not stiff—it will set overnight.
- Serve with dark chocolate sauce.

cook's note: Pistachio paste can be purchased at gourmet food shops or Middle Eastern markets.

chocolate caramel squares

On a visit home a couple of years ago, trying to think of ways to spend time with my mother, I decided it would be fun to cook together. I'd never cooked for my mom before! She let me know everything I was doing wrong with these squares—and she was right, because I burned the caramel. –*Jason*

makes 12 to 16 squares

for the bottom crust:
  1½ cups/375 mL butter
  2 cups/500 mL all-purpose flour
  ½ cup/125 ml granulated sugar

for the caramel:
  2 14 oz/398 mL cans condensed milk
  1 cup/250 mL butter
  3 tbsp/45 mL golden syrup

for the topping:
  5 cups/1.25 L milk chocolate chips

- Preheat the oven to 350°F (180°C).

crust: Cream the butter in an electric mixer then slowly add the flour and sugar to make a loose dough. Line an 8-inch (20 cm) square baking pan with parchment paper and pat the dough into the pan to form a thin layer.
- Bake in the oven for 20 minutes then set aside to cool.

caramel: Mix the condensed milk, butter, and syrup in a stainless steel bowl. Cook over a pot of boiling water, stirring occasionally with a wooden spoon, until the mixture is golden brown, then whisk until fluffy.
- Pour the caramel over the baked crust and refrigerate.

topping: Melt the chocolate in a stainless steel bowl over a pot of simmering water.
- Pour it over the firm caramel and let cool.
- When the chocolate is semi-firm, score lines on the top to form small squares. This will make it easier to cut when the chocolate is firm.
- Refrigerate until ready to serve.

cook's note: Feel free to substitute dark, semisweet, or whatever chocolate chips you prefer. If you don't have golden syrup on hand you can substitute corn syrup, although the flavour isn't as satisfying.

roasted stuffed peaches with rum and chocolate

This is another of my mother's special treats. Since my uncles were all farmers who grew fruit for Sperlari and Vergani, the great mostarda and candy-makers of Cremona, they often would bring fruit to our house. The best peaches were always for eating; the so-so ones were for baking and preserving. I loved this version because of the rum in it. –*Massimo*

serves 4

4 peaches, firm but ripe
1 cup/250 mL amaretti cookies
2 tbsp/25 mL dark rum
1 tbsp/15 mL Amaretto liqueur
4 tsp/20 mL cocoa powder
3 tsp/45 mL granulated sugar, plus
    more for dusting
Pinch salt
Butter cookies, if needed
½ cup/125 mL white wine
½ vanilla bean
2 tbsp/25 mL butter

- Preheat the oven to 450°F (230°C).

- Split the peaches in half and remove the pits. Scoop out some of the flesh to make a cavity for the stuffing and reserve.
- Pulse the reserved peach flesh, amaretti cookies, rum, liqueur, cocoa, sugar, and salt in a food processor until finely chopped. If the mixture becomes too thin, mix in a couple of butter cookies.
- Fill the peach halves with the mixture and place them in a baking dish large enough to accommodate the peaches in a single layer.
- Pour the wine around the peaches and place the vanilla bean under them. Melt the butter and drizzle it over the peaches, then sprinkle evenly with sugar.
- Bake for 15 to 20 minutes.

sticky toffee pudding with butter-rum sauce

This is a classic English dessert that's especially good in the winter, when warm and sugary is the perfect comfort. In England, "pudding" is a generic term for dessert, so don't be confused by the name: this is actually a date sponge cake covered in toffee sauce. And it's delicious. *—Michael*

serves 6

for the pudding:
1 cup/250 mL hot water
⅔ cup/150 mL chopped dates
1 tsp/5 mL baking soda
1½ cups/375 mL butter, softened
¼ cup/50 mL granulated sugar
2 eggs
⅔ cup/150 mL self-raising flour

for the sauce:
⅔ cup/150 mL butter
1½ cups/375 mL brown sugar
1 cup/250 mL whipping (35%) cream
1½ vanilla beans, split
2½ oz/75 mL dark rum

- Preheat the oven to 350°F (180°C).

pudding: Combine the water, dates, and baking soda in a bowl and let stand for 20 minutes.
- In a separate bowl, cream the butter and sugar together until light and fluffy. Gradually add the eggs, combining well. Continue to stir while slowly adding the flour, followed by the dates.
- Pour the mixture into a buttered 8-inch (20 cm) square pan. Bake in the oven for 35 to 40 minutes, or until cooked through.

sauce: In a heavy-bottomed saucepan, melt the butter over medium heat. Add the brown sugar, cream, and vanilla beans. Simmer for 6 to 10 minutes, stirring well. Stir in the rum and simmer for 2 to 3 minutes. Remove from the heat and keep warm.
- To serve, cut the pudding into squares, place them on a plate, and pour the butter-rum sauce over top.

chilled Ontario strawberry soufflé

The Ontario strawberry season is so short and precious. The best way to enjoy them is to head out to a farmer's field, pick as many as you can, then get creative—everyone loves them, whether served fresh, in jam, or in this delicious soufflé. You can easily substitute raspberries, blueberries, blackberries, or peaches, depending on the season. *–Michael*

serves 4

for the purée:
2 cups/500 mL quartered strawberries
⅓ cup/75 mL water
¼ cup/50 mL sugar
Juice of ½ lemon

for the soufflé:
4 eggs, separated
½ cup/125 mL granulated sugar
⅓ cup/75 mL water
3 gelatin leaves, soaked in water
   (or 1½ tsp/7 mL gelatin powder)
Juice of ½ lemon
⅔ cup/150 mL whipping (35%) cream
1½ cups/375 mL strawberry purée
Whipped cream, for garnish
4 small strawberries, for garnish
Grated chocolate, for garnish
Icing sugar, for garnish

purée: Combine the strawberries, water, sugar, and lemon juice in a non-reactive pan. Simmer gently for 2 to 3 minutes, stirring occasionally.
- Remove from the heat and cool. Purée in a blender and pass through a fine sieve to yield approximately 1½ cups (375 mL) of purée.

soufflé: You'll need four 4 oz (125 mL) ramekins. Tightly wrap a piece of parchment paper around each ramekin, so that it sticks up about 2 inches (5 cm) above the rim. Fasten with scotch tape.
- Place the egg yolks and sugar in a bowl over a pan of hot water and whisk until the yolks are thick and creamy.
- In a separate bowl, combine the water with the gelatin over a pan of hot water. Add the lemon juice, warming gently, and whisk until the gelatin dissolves. Cool.
- In a third bowl, whisk the cream to soft peaks. Gently fold in the strawberry purée. Pour in the egg and sugar mixture and the gelatin, then fold gently until thoroughly mixed.
- Whisk the egg whites until stiff. Add a third of the whites to the strawberry-cream mixture. Mix gently to lighten, then fold in the remaining egg whites.
- Pour into the moulds to just below the top of the parchment paper. Refrigerate for 8 hours to set.
- To serve, remove the parchment paper to reveal the soufflé. Garnish with a little whipped cream, a fresh strawberry, grated chocolate, and icing sugar.

Welsh cakes

Welsh cakes (*picau ar y maen*) are a traditional griddle cake found all over Wales, in every coffee shop and café. My son Oscar loves them and gets really excited when I say I'm in the mood to make them. They're delicious fresh off the griddle with a generous slathering of lightly chilled butter; I like them with a cup of tea at the end of the day. I don't remember where this recipe came from, but it's one I've used for many years. *–Michael*

makes 12 to 18 cakes

2 cups/500 mL all-purpose flour
2 tsp/10 mL baking powder
1¼ tsp/6 mL pumpkin pie spice
1 cup/250 mL butter
½ cup/125 mL currants
Zest of ½ lemon
½ cup/125 mL superfine sugar
2 eggs, beaten
¼ cup/50 mL milk

- Sift the flour, baking powder, and pie spice together. Rub in the butter until the mixture looks like bread crumbs. Stir in the currants, lemon zest, and sugar. Add the eggs and milk; stir to make a firm dough.
- Turn the dough onto a floured board and roll it out to ¼ inch (5 mm).
- Cook on a greased griddle or in a heavy skillet until golden brown on both sides.
- Serve hot or cold, plain or buttered.

apricot, truffle honey, and basil scones

I did a lot of my training in English hotels, where traditional afternoon tea with scones is a big thing. One day someone came into Peller talking about scones, and I said, "Only a Brit can make them properly." That became a challenge to myself to come up with something great. People tend to go with the basic, standard flavours, but I like to find different, surprising combinations. –*Jason*

makes 12 to 16 scones

2 cups/500 mL all-purpose flour
½ cup/125 mL granulated sugar
4 tsp/20 mL baking powder
1 tsp/5 mL salt
1 cup/250 mL shortening
½ cup/125 mL roughly chopped dried
  apricots
2 tbsp/25 mL truffle honey (or plain
  honey)
1 tbsp/15 mL roughly chopped basil
  leaves
½ cup/125 mL buttermilk
Icing sugar, for dusting

- Preheat the oven to 350°F (180°C).

- Combine the flour, sugar, baking powder, and salt in a large mixing bowl. Cut in the shortening to create a crumble, then fold in the dried apricots, honey, and basil. Add ¼ cup (50 mL) of the buttermilk and pull the ingredients together to make a dough.
- Wrap the dough in plastic wrap and chill until firm.
- Roll the dough out on a floured surface to 1 inch (2.5 cm) thick. Cut out 12 to 16 scones and place on a large baking sheet. Brush with the remaining buttermilk and bake for 15 to 20 minutes.
- Remove and cool on a rack. Finish with a dusting of icing sugar.

orange blossom rice pudding

You can add your own twist to this rice pudding by adding coconut, coconut milk, fresh lichees, or mango, and serving it with a scoop of ice cream or a little crème fraîche. A crispy ginger snap or almond biscotti adds a nice dimension of taste and texture. —*Michael*

serves 4 to 6

1½ cups/375 mL homogenized milk

½ cup/125 mL whipping (35%) cream

¼ tsp/1 mL salt

¼ tsp/1 mL cinnamon, plus more for garnish

1 walnut-sized piece of ginger, peeled and sliced into 4

1 cup/250 mL long grain rice

½ cup/125 mL brown sugar

1 vanilla bean, split or ½ tsp/2 mL vanilla extract

½ tsp/2 mL orange-blossom water

2 cardamom pods

¼ cup/50 mL golden raisins soaked in icewine

¼ cup/50 mL chopped toasted pistachios

Pinch cinnamon

¼ cup/50 mL plain yogurt, for garnish

- In a good-sized saucepan, combine the milk, cream, salt, cinnamon, and ginger and bring to a simmer. Add the rice and simmer gently over low heat, stirring from time to time, for 18 to 20 minutes. Once the rice has plumped up, remove it from the heat and add the sugar, vanilla, orange blossom water, and cardamom pods. Stir until the sugar has dissolved, return to the heat, and continue to cook until the rice is soft and tender. Let it sit in the saucepan for 5 minutes, then pour into a serving bowl and let cool.
- To serve, spoon the rice pudding into serving dishes. Sprinkle with the plumped raisins, chopped pistachios, and cinnamon and top with a spoonful of yogurt. Try to remove the ginger and cardamom pod before serving.

cook's note: Be sure you use long grain rice (which is light and fluffy), not short grain (which is starchy and sticky).

home-grown rhubarb and vanilla compote

Rhubarb was one of the first things I grew at our family farm: it's low maintenance and always produces lots of fruit. But it's too often overlooked by home cooks and deserves more notice. Its refreshing tartness goes well in savoury dishes, and it can be easily incorporated into many desserts. This simple preparation can be served with vanilla ice cream, crème fraîche, or whipped cream. It's also nice spooned over rice pudding or a simple sponge cake. –*Michael*

serves 4 to 6

1 lb/500 g spring rhubarb
1 cup/250 mL elderflower sparkling
  wine (non-alcoholic)
¼ cup/50 mL honey
1 walnut-sized piece of ginger, peeled
  and cut into 3
1 vanilla bean, seeds removed and
  reserved
1 tbsp/15 mL lemon juice

- Peel and trim the rhubarb stalks and cut them into 2-inch (5 cm) lengths. Heat in a shallow pot over medium-low heat with the elderflower wine, honey, ginger, vanilla seeds and bean, and the lemon juice. Bring the liquid to a simmer, then cover it with parchment paper, turn off the heat, and let it rest for 15 to 20 minutes. Turn the rhubarb and let it sit for another 15 to 20 minutes.
- Drain the liquid into a clean pot and reduce it by half, simmering gently.
- Pour it back over the rhubarb to serve.

meringue
with ice cream and marinated strawberries

Trying to explain the love I have for meringue is impossible. My mother made the best ever: fork whipped and spooned on a tray, then baked in a slow, wood-burning stove. As a young hotel cook, I made a deal with the pastry chef that I would prep his mise-en-place if he would leave some meringue and whipped cream as a snack on my return after a night out. I can make my own now, of course, and love pairing it with whatever tender fruit is in season. This one, with Ontario strawberries, is a favourite. *−Massimo*

serves 6 to 8

for the meringue:
4 egg whites
3 drops lemon juice
½ tsp/2 mL vanilla extract
1¼ cups/300 mL superfine sugar

for the strawberries:
4 cups/1 L halved strawberries
½ cup/125 mL granulated sugar
1 tsp/5 mL lemon zest
¼ cup/50 mL vodka
¼ cup/50 mL white wine

for serving:
Your favourite vanilla ice cream

- Preheat the oven to 220°F (110°C).

meringue: Place the egg whites, lemon juice, and vanilla in a bowl. Whip until stiff and gradually add two thirds of the sugar. Continue beating until the mixture forms peaks, then fold in the remaining sugar.
- Using a pastry bag, shape the meringue into 2-inch (5 cm) squares on a baking sheet lined with parchment paper.
- Bake until dry and set aside until needed.

strawberries: Combine all the ingredients in a bowl and let sit for about 10 minutes.

assembly: Place a meringue square on each plate and top with a scoop of vanilla ice cream. Press gently to create a cup and fill it with strawberries. Cover with another square, then repeat the process: ice cream, strawberries, and meringue.

cook's note: If you like, add a little whipped cream to each meringue.

tender fruit, rosemary, and vanilla strudel

Years ago, while waiting for a visa to go to Bermuda, I worked for Steve Treadwell in Niagara on the Lake, filling in as pastry chef with some recipes left behind by the previous guy. I didn't have much pastry experience, but one day I was struck by the simplicity of an apple pie recipe: fruit, sugar, and starch. I suddenly realized that baking was just like any other kind of cooking, where basic concepts can be transferred to all kinds of ingredients. Ever since, I've been playing around with dressed-up tender fruit in various recipes. This strudel has become a real favourite. *–Jason*

serves 8 to 10

1 cup/250 mL sliced peaches
1 cup/250 mL sliced plums
1 cup/250 mL sliced apricots
1 cup/250 mL pitted cherries
1 cup/250 mL diced sponge cake
¼ cup/50 mL cornstarch
½ cup/125 mL granulated sugar
2 vanilla beans
2 tbsp/25 mL chopped rosemary
1 sheet puff pastry
1 egg yolk, beaten with 1 tbsp/15 mL water

- Preheat the oven to 400°F (200°C).

- Mix the peaches, plums, apricots, cherries, and diced sponge cake in a large bowl. Add the cornstarch, ¼ cup (50 mL) of the sugar, seeds from one vanilla bean, and 1 tbsp (15 mL) of the rosemary.
- On a lightly floured surface, roll out the pastry into a 12 x 9-inch (30 x 22 cm) rectangle.
- Place the filling in a line along one long side of the puff pastry, leaving a 1-inch (2.5 cm) border. Brush the egg along the edges of the pastry and bring the dough over the fruit. Pinch the ends and fold them underneath. Using a sharp knife, cut slits in the top of the strudel to allow steam to escape and to make cutting easier after baking.
- Combine the remaining sugar, vanilla seeds, and rosemary. Brush the strudel with the last of the egg and sprinkle with the sugar mixture.
- Bake for 15 minutes or until golden, then cover with foil, if necessary, to prevent it from burning, and bake for another 10 minutes. Remove from the oven and rest for 10 minutes on a wire rack.
- Cut along the lines in the dough and serve.

strawberry, rhubarb, and lemon tart

I love lemon tart but rarely get to make it: at Peller we try to limit our ingredients to what's locally available, and we can't grow lemons in southern Ontario (yet). So I make my tarts from other fruit (although I do still sneak in some lemon). When I worked at the Millcroft Inn, we made lots of jams, and some of the flavour combinations I developed there have made their way into my fruit tarts. You can make them small or large, or prepare them on a tray and cut them into squares. *–Jason*

serves 8 to 10

for the tart shells:
3 cups/750 mL all-purpose flour
1¼ cups/300 mL icing sugar
1 cup/250 mL butter
2 eggs
Zest of 1 lemon
1 vanilla bean

for the filling:
9 cups/2.25 L fresh strawberries
3 cups/750 mL rhubarb
1 cup/250 mL lemon juice
½ cup/125 mL thinly sliced lemon zest
1 cup/250 mL granulated sugar
¼ cup/50 mL cornstarch
1 tbsp/15 mL vanilla extract

- Preheat the oven to 350°F (180°C).

tart shells: Sift the flour and icing sugar together into a bowl then knead the butter into the flour.
- In a separate bowl, mix the eggs, lemon zest, and vanilla seeds then add them to the flour until a dough forms. Wrap the dough with plastic wrap and refrigerate for at least 1 hour.
- Roll the chilled dough out to ¼ inch (5 mm) thick and line two 9-inch (23 cm) tart shells. Refrigerate the shells for at least 15 minutes, then bake for 18 to 20 minutes.

filling: Heat all the ingredients in a large pot over high heat and cook until the mixture becomes a purée. Pour it into the pre-baked tart shells and rest the tarts on the counter for 10 minutes before moving them to the refrigerator to chill.

index

whitecap

Jesse Marchand: production manager
Jeffrey Bryan: publicity coordinator
Michelle Furbacher: art director
Taryn Boyd: managing editor
Robert McCullough: publisher

madison

Dwight Allott: illustrations
Ian Garlick.com: food photographs
Felicity Barnum-Bobb & Simon Daley: food & prop styling except for
Valentina Harris: food styling pp. 13, 14, 17, 43, 48, 51, 65, 69, 70, 102–03, 163, 191, 194–95, 204, 213, 222, 254–55, 259, 264, 267, 268, 271
Evan Dion: chefs photograph p. viii
Joanne Tsakos Photography: chefs photographs, pp. xvi, 21, 25, 26, 56, 61, 85, 86, 126, 152, 178, 216, 236, 251
Garrison McArthur Photographers: Michael Bonacini photographs pp. 37 and 48 right
J.P. Moczulski: Massimo Capra photograph p. 122 right
Meg Parsons: Jason Parsons photograph p. 174 right
Alicia Hogan: chefs photography, pp. 52, 122, and 174 left, 282, 285, 288
Lesley Fraser: editing
Ruth Pincoe: index
Sharon Kish: interior design & layout
Brendan Davis: production manager
Oliver Salzmann: publisher